THE SEARCH FOR THE LOST RECTORS

reflections on the history of Old Christ Churh and Pensacola in the nineteenth century

A West Florida Pioneer Series Book

THE SEARCH FOR THE LOST RECTORS

reflections on the history of Old Christ Churh and Pensacola in the nineteenth century

by BEVERLY MADISON CURRIN, Ph.D
Rector, Christ Church
Pensacola, Florida

a venture of the University of
West Florida Foundation
Pensacola

The SEARCH for the LOST RECTORS by Beverly Madison Currin, Ph.D.
© 1999 • by the University of West Florida Foundation, Inc.
All rights reserved

Printed in the United States of America

ISBN: 0-9659142-2-4

ଏ⊛

Library of Congress Catalog Card Number: 98-061612

TABLE OF CONTENTS

THE PROLOGUE 3

PART ONE—What Gary Saw 7

PART TWO—History of Old Christ Church 15
    The Early Years 17
    Christ Church is Organized 20
    A Church Building Constructed on Seville Square 22
    The First Rectors 23
    John Jackson Scott and a New Age Dawns 25

PART THREE—History of Old Christ Church, 1855-1867 35
    The Gathering Storm 37
    Fort Sumter and the War Begins 39
    The Exiles Return 43

PART FOUR—History of Old Christ Church, 1867-1997 49
    The Dawning of a New Age 51
    Old Christ Church in the Twentieth Century 62
    The Return of Old Christ Church to Its Original Owner 67

PART FIVE—The Search for the Lost Rectors, 1988 71
    Search for the Lost Rectors, An Archaeological
        Investigation 73
    The Groundbreaking Ceremony, May 14, 1988 75

2 THE SEARCH FOR THE LOST RECTORS

The Archaeological Investigation Begins, May 16, 1988 78
Burial Chamber I Discovered, May 17, 1988 78
Burial Chamber II Discovered, May 31, 1988 82
Burial Chamber III Discovered, June 13, 1988 85
Identification of the Skeletal Remains, July 8, 1988 86
Funeral Preparations 87
The Funeral Service, July 23, 1988 89

PART SIX—The Lost Rectors 91
Joseph Hubbard Saunders, 1800-1839 93
Frederick Foote Peake, 1809-1846 104
David Dubois Flower, 1822-1853 110

SOURCES AND ACKNOWLEDGMENTS 115

INDEX 119

The Prologue

This book has been more than thirty years in the making. It really began when I became rector of Christ Church in 1966, starting a long love affair with Old Christ Church on Seville Square, the home of Christ Church for most of the nineteenth century. In 1903, the congregation moved from the old church building on Seville Square, built in 1832, to the present church building at Wright and Palafox streets.

Two recent events provided the occasion for this book: *The Search for the Lost Rectors*, an archaeological dig under the old church in 1988 and more recently the beginning of the restoration of the old church building following its return to Christ Church from the city of Pensacola in 1996. The story of its return is included in this book.

The book is divided into several sections. We begin with the incredible story of what Gary Powell saw after the archaeological dig was completed and during the funeral service for the three "lost rectors" on June 23, 1988. Then we have the history of Christ Church, which began in 1764 when the first Anglican missionaries were sent to Pensacola by the Bishop of London. Following that is the story of the founding of Christ Church in 1827 and the construction of the church building in 1832. The history of Christ

Church in the nineteenth century is written against the background of the history of Pensacola and Northwest Florida, including the Civil War years, the hardships of Reconstruction, and the development and growth of Christ Church and Pensacola through the turn of the century.

The next section, "The Search for the Lost Rectors," is a fascinating story of what happened, how it happened, and the amazing conclusions of that archaeological investigation under the direction of Dr. Judy Bense of the University of West Florida, one of the nation's leading archaeologists. More than just three "lost rectors" were found during that archaeological investigation. What else was found is also included in this section of the book.

Then you will find the biographies of the three lost rectors. They were buried under the old church between 1839 and 1853. Included in this section is information never before published.

Both the archaeological dig, called by the media "The Search for the Lost Rectors," and what Gary saw became the catalyst that convinced me that God's challenge to me, as the sixteenth rector of Christ Church, was to support and promote the restoration of the oldest church building in Florida. This really is "holy ground," and when you read this book, you will understand.

One note about yellow fever, which took the lives of two of the rectors and which caused so many deaths over the years. In the nineteenth century, the cause of yellow fever was not known. For that reason, those who died of yellow fever were buried as soon as possible. It was not until the twentieth century that it was discovered that yellow fever was a virus carried by the *Aedes aegypti* mosquito. There was no known cure. Almost every summer, Pensacola had its share of yellow fever cases and sometimes it reached epidemic proportions due to the hot, wet climate of the Gulf Coast.

As you read these pages you will discover that many of those who built Christ Church were the same citizens who built Pensacola from a small town to a major city of the New South. These were people with vision,

PROLOGUE

hope, faith, and fortitude.

Today, let us hope that as we come into a deeper appreciation of our past, we will be better able to follow in the footsteps of those who came before us as we move into the twenty-first century.

Beverly Madison Currin, Ph.D.
Rector, Christ Church
Pensacola, Florida

Old Christ Church, after 1879. (Courtesy of Christ Church Archives)

†

PART ONE

What Gary Saw

PART ONE
What Gary Saw

"Then one of the elders addressed me, saying, 'Who are these, clothed in white robes, and whence have they come?' I said to him, 'Sir, you know.' And he said to me, 'These are they who have come out of the great tribulation; they have washed their robes and made them white in the blood of the Lamb. Therefore are they before the throne of God, and serve him day and night within his temple; and he who sits upon the throne will shelter them with his presence. They shall hunger no more, neither thirst anymore; the sun shall not strike them, nor any scorching heat. For the Lamb in the midst of the throne will be their shepherd, and he will guide them to springs of living water; and God will wipe away every tear from their eyes.'" (Rev. 7: 13-17).

THE BIBLE IS FULL OF STORIES OF THE BEYOND IN THE MIDDLE OF HUMAN life, those rare and mystical moments in the lives of human beings when the veil between this world and the next is drawn aside, those mystical moments when the past and the future invade the present. Some background is necessary at this point even though it is more fully recorded later in this book.

During the Civil War, a legend was born, and that legend was that while Pensacola was occupied by the Union Army and Christ Church was used as a barracks, hospital, and jail, a young boy saw the soldiers dig up the three priests who had been buried under the floor of the church between 1839 and 1853. They were looking for valuables. In 1988, Christ Church and the University of West Florida conducted an archaeological investigation to determine if these three former rectors were still buried where they were supposed to be. They were, and after the investigation was over, a funeral service was held for the three rectors much as it must have been conducted so many years ago. Something wonderful and mystical happened much like the passage of Holy Scripture quoted at the beginning of this chapter, and it concerns what Gary Powell saw.

This mystical moment happened on July 23, 1988, during the funeral procession for the burial of the three rectors. I did not know what Gary had seen for several weeks. He thought that everybody else had seen what he had seen. He did not know the significance of what he had seen, and because of that he said nothing about it. We did not realize the importance of what he had seen until he read his term paper. Gary wanted to check to be certain he was using the right terms for those who participated in the funeral service.

Gary is an exceptional person, a brilliant young man who was injured in an accident several years before "the search for the lost rectors." He has a photographic memory and is a quadriplegic, confined to a wheelchair. With help from his family and friends, he was a student at the University of West Florida in the summer of 1988, taking a summer school course in archaeology.

Gary was very much present at the funeral that warm, clear Saturday morning at Old Christ Church. He had worked long and hard on the project that late spring and early summer. He was there every day, making notes, asking questions and writing a weekly summary of what had happened. Each of the students had to work in some capacity with the archaeologists, and since Gary could not do that kind of work, he had been assigned the task of keeping the records. Each student had to submit a final paper, and Gary chose to write the story of "The Search for the Lost Rectors," concluding with a description of the funeral.

At the end of the term, Dr. Judy Bense, the archeologist in charge of the

PART ONE, What Gary Saw

project and the teacher of the summer school class, had a picnic at her house. After dinner, Gary, my wife Eleanor, Judy, Gary's mother, and I were having a visit. Gary asked if he could read his account of the funeral and if I would help him with some of the names and titles of the participants since he was not an Episcopalian and not fully conversant with their titles.

And so he read us that part of his paper about the funeral. He had written the following: "The crucifer led the procession out of the church."

"Is that the correct term?" Gary asked. I told him crucifer was correct.

Then he continued: "The crucifer led the procession out of the church, followed by the choir of Christ Church, followed by Dr. Currin, the rector of Christ Church, and Dr. Morris Marx, the president of the university,"

"So far, so good," I told Gary.

Then Gary continued reading: "They were followed by the three church clergymen and then the pallbearers with the three caskets containing the remains of the three lost rectors." I was dumbfounded . . . The "three church clergymen." Who were they? What had he seen? There was no one behind Morris Marx and me except the pallbearers carrying the caskets!

Dr. Currin conducts funeral service for the lost rectors on July 23, 1988. Gary Powell (seated in wheelchair) is a member of the assembled congregation. (Photo by Gary McCracken, courtesy of Pensacola News Journal)

Had Gary made a simple mistake? Or had he seen something we had been unable to see? Those of us listening to Gary leaned forward. The others had caught it too. The three church clergymen. I asked him to read this again. He did. It was the same the second time. The three church clergymen were still there in his paper. I asked him to repeat it a third time and to describe everything he saw in more detail. We all waited with bated breath. He repeated it the same way, but this time he asked me, "Who where the three men in white robes? What do you call them, church clergymen? What were their titles?" I asked him to describe them. He seemed surprised. "You saw them. Why do you ask?"

I said, "Gary, tell me exactly what you saw. Remember we were in front. They were behind us. What did they look like? What were they wearing?"

Gary described them for me. "One was shorter than the other two, and one was quite tall. One had on those old antique eyeglasses down on his nose. They were walking side by side. One had a big black book in his hand. Two were laughing, and one was very serious. They were dressed in white. They didn't have any shoes on. I thought that was very strange." And then he added, "After we got down the side street and into the backyard of the church, I did not see them anymore. Who were they?"

I told him there were no three men in white robes behind Dr. Marx and me. He insisted they were there. He asked for the photo album with the pictures of the funeral, and when he looked through the pictures, he was surprised and puzzled. "But they were there. I saw them. I know I did."

I told Gary I was convinced he did see them, even if none of the rest of us did. I told Gary I fully believed they were there and that for some reason God had enabled him to see something we had not seen. Again he asked me, "But Dr. Currin, who were they?"

I replied to him, "Gary you know, and I do too."

He looked at me in wonder and said, "I feel so honored that God let me see them."

Gary's mother, who had been with him at the funeral, said, "Now I know why he kept asking me after the service began where the three men in white had gone. I had no idea what he was talking about, but he contin-

PART ONE, What Gary Saw

ued looking around trying to find something."

Later when I visited Gary at his house, he told me with a twinkle in his eye, "The reason you did not see them is that you were not looking."

What does this mean? Maybe it means that at times, and for those with the eyes to see, the veil between this world and the next is very thin indeed. Maybe this is what the church means by the Communion of Saints. Maybe it means that the Kingdom of God really is in our midst, in the middle of our lives. Maybe this is partly what Jesus meant when he said, "You who have eyes to see, look around you."

God has indeed surrounded us with a great cloud of witnesses so that we can rejoice in their fellowship and run with endurance the race that is set before us. And it means, too, that Jesus was right, "Blessed are the pure in heart, for they shall see God." And Gary really is the pure in heart.

Some time later, while reflecting on this, I remembered that when Moses saw the burning bush and the presence of God, he took off his shoes because he was on holy ground. And then and there, I realized that it was my responsibility to try to get Old Christ Church back in the hands of the church wardens and vestrymen of Christ Church. I realized it was my responsibility to try to get that wonderful old historic building restored. After all, it is holy ground, and the three priests who made "The Search for the Lost Rectors" possible are buried under that grand old building. Gary Powell and the "three church clergymen" made me understand just that.

PART TWO

History of Old Christ Church

1763 - 1855

PART TWO
History of Old Christ Church in the Nineteenth Century

THE EARLY YEARS

THE HISTORY OF CHRIST CHURCH GOES BACK TO THE middle of the eighteenth century, long before the construction of the original church building in 1832 on Seville Square. Following the Treaty of Paris in 1763, when Spain relinquished ownership of West Florida to the British, the Bishop of London commissioned the Rev. William Dawson to bring the Church of England to Pensacola. Dawson was commissioned on July 2, 1764. His task was to minister to the British subjects in Pensacola and to administer the rites of the Church. He arrived in Pensacola the following year and began his work in a community which had previously allowed only the Roman Catholic Church as the official religion.

The Rev. Mr. Dawson did not stay long and was followed by the Rev. Nathaniel Cotton. Cotton wrote the Bishop of London on June 10, 1770, and thanked him for sending prayer books, Bibles, and religious tracts. He also wrote that births had exceeded burials in Pensacola, and that between 1768 and 1770, he had buried sixty-four people and had baptized eighty-two children. He also recommended that schoolmasters in Holy Orders be appointed in the colonies because there were only two clergymen in the province.

The early British missionaries sent by the Bishop of London found no church buildings remaining from the Spanish occupation. But some important things did remain, especially the Presidio San Miguel. As early as 1765, surveyor Elias Durnford designed a community around the old San Miguel stockade and renamed it Fort Pensacola. The design of the town surrounded a public square or stockade which today is the Pensacola historic district at Seville Square. Archaeological investigations have identified remnants of the foundations of government buildings constructed there during the British period. Durnford's town plan for Pensacola called for wide streets with good-sized lots in order for each owner to have a garden. Today, Garden Street in downtown Pensacola is a reminder of our English heritage.

The Rev. George Chapman was the last Anglican priest appointed by the Bishop of London as a missionary of the Church of England for Pensacola. These missionary efforts of the Church of England were brought to an end when West Florida was returned to Spain in 1781. The British had little time, less than twenty years, for their missionary work in West Florida and Pensacola in particular. However seeds had been sown, and some years later they would bear fruit.

Spanish Florida was soon divided into East Florida, with St. Augustine as the capital, and West Florida, with Pensacola as the capital. West Florida extended to the west along the Gulf to the Pearl River, north to the mouth of the Yazoo River, east to the Chattahoochee River, and down the Apalachicola River to the Gulf of Mexico. That would be an area stretching from New Orleans north to Natchez, across to Columbus, Georgia, and south to Apalachicola, Florida, including, of course, all of the present Panhandle.

When Spain regained West Florida in 1781, many of the English names of streets in Pensacola were changed. George Street became Palafox; Mansfield Street was renamed Zaragoza; Granby and Harcourt streets became Intendencia; Prince Street was renamed Romana; Johnston became Barcelona; Charlotte Street became Alcaniz; Cumberland was changed to Baylen; York was renamed Florida Blanca; and Lindsey was changed to Reus. Fort George on Gage Hill became known as Fort San Miguel but later regained its original name. The great plaza in the center of town took the name Ferdinand VII in honor of the reigning Spanish monarch. This second Spanish period was more progressive than the first, but the English had laid the foundations of a town and Pensacola began to grow.

Then came Andrew Jackson. The general was no stranger to West Florida. In the 1803 Louisiana Treaty, there was no reference to Spanish West Florida, but the United States claimed the territory as far east as the present-day Florida and Alabama border. During the War of 1812, Jackson invaded Florida but his major victory was the defeat of the Red Stick (Creek) forces at Horseshoe Bend (Alabama) in the spring of 1814. The British had also arrived in Florida. To confuse matters even more, the Spanish, who were allied with England in the Peninsular War against Napoleon, had given permission for the British to occupy Fort San Miguel and Fort Barrancas in Pensacola. Jackson entered Pensacola, and to keep from provoking war with Spain, said he was protecting Spanish neutrality. He entered Pensacola on November 7, 1814. When the British retreated to Barrancas, Jackson followed. The British then attempted to destroy the fort and left Pensacola to Jackson who then returned the city to the Spanish.

Jackson's second visit to Pensacola came in 1818 in an attempt to take the city from the Spanish peaceably if possible, but he made it clear he would take it by force if necessary. The city was taken by Jackson, and Fort Barrancas was stormed by the American forces. The Spanish surrendered. Jackson sent his prisoners to Cuba and appointed a civil and military governor for Pensacola. He then went home to Tennessee.

On February 22, 1819, the Adams-Onis Treaty was signed, which provided for the Floridas to be transferred to the United States. President James Monroe appointed General Jackson as the commissioner to receive East and West Florida from Spain and to serve as the first governor. At first he declined, but a delegation arrived at the Hermitage urging him to accept, and friends in Washington also encouraged him to go to Florida. Giving up his commission on June 1, 1821, at Montpelier, Alabama, he now had to wait for word that the Spanish in Pensacola were ready to turn the government over to him.

Days passed, and still not receiving word from Pensacola, Jackson entered Florida with the U.S. Fourth Infantry and stopped at the home of Manuel Gonzalez, which was about fifteen miles from the city. On June 28, with Jackson staying outside the city, he sent his wife, Rachel, to Pensacola where she remained at the home of Dr. John Brosnaham. The basis of the delay at this point was that the Spanish Governor expected Jackson to call on him while Jackson expected the Spanish Governor to call on him.

On July 10, Jackson accepted the transfer of East Florida, and finally plans were approved for the change of command ceremony in Pensacola for 10 a.m. on July 17, 1821, in Plaza Ferdinand. The Spanish flag was lowered. The Stars and Stripes rose above the crowded plaza. All of Florida was now a Territory of the United States.

With the Spanish gone, religious freedom was now granted. Pensacola began to grow. From an estimated one thousand inhabitants in 1821, the town doubled in size in ten years. Many of those moving into Pensacola were not Roman Catholic, making the area ripe for missionaries.

CHRIST CHURCH IS ORGANIZED

In response to this need, the General Missionary Society of the Episcopal Church sent the first Episcopal missionary to Pensacola in 1827. The Rev. Ralph Williston stopped by Pensacola for three weeks on his way from New Orleans to Tallahassee. Perhaps it was an exaggeration, but he wrote, "The whole of the American population and many of the Roman Catholics attended divine services." He reported that he had conducted seven baptisms and one marriage. He also reported that he found twelve Episcopalians, ten Methodists, two Baptists and two Presbyterians.

Williston called a meeting at the court house on June 4, 1827, for the purpose of "embodying and collecting public sentiment upon the subject of establishing a Protestant Church." Those who attended the meeting organized the "Protestant Association in the City of Pensacola" and determined that the association would organize a Protestant Episcopal Church. Why an Episcopal Church when the Methodists had been in Pensacola working for the same purpose? Was it because the Episcopal Church was closer to what the community had known during the years of Spanish influence when the Roman Catholic Church was the only church allowed? The Episcopal liturgy was similar to the Roman Catholic liturgy in many respects, and the Church of England had been in Pensacola years before. The Episcopal Church also had the apostolic succession with bishops, priests, and deacons.

The Protestant Association elected a vestry to govern the temporal affairs of the newly organized church. Those elected were Com. Melanchton T. Woolsey, commandant of the Navy Yard; along with Henry Wilson; Silvester Bill; S.R. Overton; M. Crupper; John Jerrison; and Robert Mitchell.

Commodore Woolsey was authorized to solicit subscriptions to construct a church building. The Hon. Joseph M. White, territorial delegate to the Congress of 1825, purchased land on Seville Square for $1,500, a large sum for those days. He then sold the property to the vestry for $400. Then the vestry petitioned the Legislative Council of the Territory of Florida to incorporate Christ's Church. On October 14, the Territorial Legislature approved the Articles of Incorporation. Two days later, Gov. William P. Duval signed the incorporation into effect. That same year, the General Missionary Society sent the Rev. Addison Searle to be in charge of the parish. Remaining only a few months, he was followed by the Rev. Benjamin Hutchins of Philadelphia.

A CHURCH BUILDING CONSTRUCTED ON SEVILLE SQUARE

The Rev. Benjamin Hutchins continued raising funds to construct a church building, obtaining $500 from the Domestic and Foreign Missionary Society and $400 from interested friends. Those efforts, together with funds already raised by Commodore Woolsey and the vestry, enabled construction of the church building to begin. The building was completed in 1832 at a cost of $4,500 with a debt of $2,363.

The church building centered on Seville Square and overlooked Pensacola Bay. It was Norman-Gothic in design and rectangular in shape. Built of local brick and plaster with a two-tiered square tower, the exterior was ornamented with battlements and surmounted by a cross. The building had arched neoclassic clear glass windows with a large fan light window over the main door. An organ loft was at the east end of the building. The pews had doors which were later removed by action of the vestry. There was a door at the rear of the altar, connecting the church building with a sacristy and vestry room.

Following Hutchins was the Rev. Ashbel Steele of Saybrook, Connecticut, assigned to Christ Church by the General Missionary Society. He arrived in Pensacola in November 1833. He brought $2,000 from friends in the East. Steele ministered to his own flock as well as to those at the Navy Yard and the city's African-Americans, both free and slave.

THE FIRST RECTORS

Steele was followed by the Rev. Joseph Hubbard Saunders in 1836. Saunders became the first rector of the parish, those before him being missionary priests assigned to Pensacola by the General Missionary Society of the Episcopal Church. The parish was now self-supporting even though it would continue to face financial troubles for many years to come. Joseph Saunders, a scholar by nature, was a native of North Carolina and was interested in the call to Pensacola because the parish was not only looking for a rector but one who would help fulfill the parish's desire for the establishment of a school for the youth of the city.

The church building was consecrated by the Rt. Rev. Jackson Kemper, Missionary Bishop of Missouri and Indiana, on the First Sunday in Lent, March 4, 1838, during a short visit while he was on his way from New Orleans to Tallahassee. The Rev. Joseph Saunders also took a leadership position in the founding of the Diocese of Florida at the Primary Conven-

PART TWO, History of Old Christ Church

tion held at St. John's Episcopal Church in Tallahassee in 1838. Saunders was the presiding officer. The Lay Delegates to the Primary Convention from Christ Church were Judge John A. Cameron, Thomas M. Blount, and Edwin Drake, all three of whom rose to prominence not only in the church but in the community as well. Judge Cameron drafted the Constitution and Canons of the new diocese. The seven founding churches were Christ Church, Pensacola; St. John's Church, Tallahassee; Trinity Church,

Old Christ Church as it originally appeared (Courtesy of Christ Church Archives).

St. Augustine; Trinity Church, Apalachicola; St. Joseph's Church, St. Joseph; St. John's Church, Jacksonville; and St. Paul's Church, Key West.

Joseph Saunders reported to the Diocese of Florida in his annual parish report that Christ Church was the only Protestant church in the community and that he had ministered to the entire Protestant population. He had a ministry at the Navy Yard and a Sunday afternoon service for the African Americans during which the members of the parish gave up their pews and sat in the balcony.

During his time as rector, many Christ Church parishioners entered public service, becoming leading citizens of Pensacola. Walker Anderson was clerk of the vestry, a delegate to Diocesan Convention time and time again, chief justice of the Supreme Court of Florida, and a delegate to the General Convention of the Episcopal Church. His son, William Edward Anderson, who followed in his father's footsteps as a leader in the parish, was also the first mayor of Pensacola under the city charter. Benjamin Drake Wright was a member of the Legislative Council of the Territory of Florida, U.S. district attorney for West Florida, chief justice of the Supreme Court and, for many years, editor of the *Pensacola Gazette*.

The Rev. Joseph Saunders died of yellow fever on October 24, 1839, and was buried that same afternoon. A portion of the floor of the vestry room was removed, and he was buried under the place where he had sat at vestry meetings.

Following his tragic death, the parish was without a rector for three years, but from time to time the Rev. Rodman Lewis, an Episcopal priest and chaplain for the U.S. Army at Fort Barrancas, held services and ministered to the congregation.

In 1842 the vestry called the Rev. Frederick Foote Peake, a graduate of the General Theological Seminary in New York City who had been ordained to the priesthood by Bishop Jackson Kemper. At the time of his call, Peake was rector of Christ Church in St. Louis, Missouri. He was suffering from a serious lung disorder and thought a change in climate might help. One of his interests, like his predecessor, was the education of youth, and the vestry wanted him to work in this capacity as well as serve as rector of the parish.

Shortly after his arrival, he established the Pensacola Collegiate Institute, the purpose of which was to educate the city's youth without regard to religious affiliation. The school and parish grew under his able leadership, but his lung condition worsened and he died of consumption on November 27, 1846, having been in Pensacola only four years. Again the floor of the church building was removed, and he was buried beside the Rev. Joseph Saunders. He was succeeded by his brother, the Rev. Charles Foote Peake, who had come to Pensacola to help him during his final months of illness. He remained in Pensacola only a short time before going to Eutaw, Alabama.

During these years, again many leading parishioners continued to become leaders in the community. Among them were Hyer, Anderson, Knowles, Garnier, Baker, Barkley, Campbell, Chase, Dorr, Gage, Bell, Strong, Brosnaham and Avery, to name but a few.

JOHN JACKSON SCOTT AND A NEW AGE DAWNS

In 1848, the vestry called the Rev. John Jackson Scott, rector of St. Paul's Episcopal Church in Quincy, Florida, where he was in the midst of a controversy over the temperance movement. According to Joseph Cushman's book, *A Goodly Heritage*, Scott, like many good Episcopalians, saw nothing wrong with St. Paul's admonition that "a little wine is good for the stomach" (1 Timothy 5:23). When the local Methodist missionary attacked Scott and tried to dry up Gadsden County, he took to his pulpit, calling the Temperance Society "baptized infidelity" and suggested that the clergy ought to preach more Christ and less prohibition.

At that point, John Jackson Scott accepted the call of the vestry and moved to Pensacola. He would continue as rector of Christ Church until his retirement forty years later in 1889, except for stints as a chaplain in the U.S. Army at Fort Barrancas and later in Mobile.

Scott was an Anglo-Catholic, holding a high church view of the one holy catholic and apostolic church and the priesthood. He was an imposing man, tall and large and outspoken. In his first Annual Report to the Diocese of Florida in 1848, he wrote, "Services on Wednesdays and Fridays weekly, until the rubric is complied with, by daily services offering a continual approach to God in the place where He has promised to be present." The rubric was in the 1789 Book of Common Prayer, which called for weekly celebrations of the Holy Communion especially on high holy days.

He was born at Rose Dew, a plantation near Beaufort, South Carolina, probably in 1815, the county residence of his parents in St. Luke's parish. His father was a native of Scotland and his mother's family were Swiss Huguenots. He graduated from the College of William and Mary in Williamsburg, Virginia. He also graduated from the Virginia Theological Seminary in 1839, the year of Joseph Saunders' death. He never mentioned his birth date in any of his writings, and the date of his birth is not on his tombstone at St. John's Cemetery in Pensacola. However, from the Archives of the College of William and Mary, we find that when he signed the matriculation book in 1834, he indicated he was nineteen years of age. When he signed the book the following year, he listed his age as twenty. So, it is safe to assume that he was born in 1815, making him thirty-three years of age when he became rector of Christ Church.

According to the *Southern Churchman* of July 19, 1839, Scott was ordained deacon at St. Paul's Church, Alexandria, Virginia, by the Rt. Rev. Richard Channing Moore, Bishop of Virginia, on Thursday morning, July 11. He was ordained to the priesthood by the Rt. Rev. Leonidas Polk, Bishop of Louisiana, at Christ Church (now Christ Church Cathedral) in New Orleans on March 24, 1841.

Scott began his ministry in Livingston, Alabama, where he organized and established St. James' Church. From there he went to Quincy, Florida. Early in his ministry in Pensacola, Columbia College in New York City (now Columbia University) conferred upon him the S.T.D. degree, and in later years, he was given the honorary LL.D. degree by the College of William and Mary.

For many years the nation was sharply divided over slavery, states' rights, federalism, and tariff arguments, all of which pitted Northern manufactur-

PART TWO, History of Old Christ Church

ing interests against Southern planters and slave owners. Beginning in 1828, the Tariff of Abominations caused outright confrontation between the federal government and state's rights. John C. Calhoun of South Carolina had served as vice president during Andrew Jackson's first term in the White

The Rev. John Jackson Scott, rector 1848-1889. (Courtesy of Christ Church Archives).

House, but became a sharp critic of Jackson during the 1828 election. By 1832, Calhoun was a U.S. senator from South Carolina and was in the process of devising plans of secession. Under the surface, the South was headed for just that. These issues had great effect on Scott. His first five years at Christ Church were difficult ones.

Scott was a great admirer of John C. Calhoun and wrote about the man at the time of his death. Both Calhoun and Scott were South Carolinians. Calhoun had supported President James Madison in the War of 1812. President John Monroe appointed him secretary of war. Later as Andrew Jackson's vice president, he appeared certain to succeed Jackson in 1832. That did not happen. One reason may have been his deep concern for both South Carolina and the South in general. Calhoun felt that the interests of the South were different from the rest of the nation and that these interests were being ignored outside the South. Furthermore, Calhoun believed that any state had the right to nullify any law which threatened its well-being. He hoped that this policy could and would prevent revolution.

Having resigned the vice presidency, Calhoun then entered the U.S. Senate, spending the rest of his life trying to further the interests of the South in general and South Carolina in particular. Perhaps it was Calhoun's goal to look out for minority interests that led Scott to admire him so much. In his later years, Calhoun pled for union and the rightful place of the South in that union, but he was generally misunderstood. His last words before his death were, "The South, the poor South."

Antebellum Pensacola was growing, but was still subject to the nation's boom and bust cycles. Roads were connecting Pensacola with other towns and cities. William Henry Chase, a communicant of Christ Church, a graduate of West Point, and an engineer and financial genius, arrived in Pensacola in 1826. Chase worked for years developing the city and serving on the vestry of Christ Church. He built Fort Pickens in 1834, Fort McRee in 1839 and Fort Barrancas in 1844. Federal money was coming into the city as were the military in defense of the Navy Yard. The Bank of Pensacola came into being due to the efforts of Chase in 1833. The economy was soon boosted by the timber trade, naval stores, and the export of cotton.

PART TWO, History of Old Christ Church

Railroad expansion began with plans to connect Pensacola with Alabama and Georgia.

Disaster struck in 1837. In a national financial panic, the Bank of Pensacola failed, but the city continued to grow and develop. In 1856, Capt. Chase resigned his commission in order to serve full time as president of the new Alabama and Florida Railroad with the hope of making Pensacola a center for the export of cotton and timber. Slave labor was used for the construction of roads, railroads, and forts surrounding the city. Only a few miles outside Pensacola, the community of Bagdad became the home of the largest textile factory in the state. These years also saw the expansion of religious influence in the city from both the Protestant and Roman Catholic churches.

Florida was admitted to the Union in 1845 as the twenty-seventh state with Florida as a slave state and Iowa admitted next as a free state. In the 1850s, Steven Russell Mallory of Pensacola, who was U.S. senator from Florida, promoted shipbuilding and the expansion of the Navy Yard. Mallory, under the Confederacy, later become Secretary of the Navy. During the years before the outbreak of war, always beneath the surface was the burning question of slavery and states' rights.

Scott gave the following description of Christ Church soon after his arrival in Pensacola: "We have a neat church edifice of brick with a tower surmounted with a cross. It is beautifully situated, and whether you approach the city by land or water, almost the first object that meets the eye is the emblem of our salvation, glittering under the beams of the sun and unobscured when the tempest sweeps the sky. It serves to arrest the attention, and fix it on Jesus, who poured out the blood of cleansing for sinning on a similar instrument."

Upon learning of the death of John C. Calhoun, Scott wrote: "We are in possession of a report of Mr. Calhoun's death, and I fear it is so indeed. Though it would not have been unexpected from his age and sickness, yet it is sad news, and I feel as if I had been deprived of one whose place never can be supplied in this life of mine. Many a pilgrim from the soil of South Carolina who like myself stands unconnected with the strifes of parties, will be sad, and mourn and weep, as he realized the fact, that the great man of our common country, and the man who had not his superior on earth for mental endorsement is now dead. It will require time for the feelings to recover from the calamity which has fallen on South Carolina and the nation. When time shall pass and utterance shall begin the great man who has been too frequently abused and wronged by the ill judging will begin to be appreciated and his patriotism, his love of the country and his devotion to the Constitution will become as common themes for eulogy, as it is now and has been for many days his gigantic interest."

While serving the parish of Christ Church, Dr. Scott began a mission church in Warrington—St. John's—and in 1851 it was added to the roles of the Diocese of Florida. At the same time, the hard-working rector was doing missionary work in Blackwater (Milton), but a church would not be officially established there until after the Civil War.

Toward the end of his first five years as rector, Scott recorded that he could not continue working in Warrington, writing that "I have hardly found a community of church people knowing so little of the character and destiny of the church and of the obligations and duties of churchmen." Later he wrote, "I am not anxious to remain here, unless it be the will of God, and from the small support and no desire to make it move, I see His will bidding me to do what I can quickly, and to remove to some other place, that this post may be occupied by a single man whom it would suit." And then he added: "I for one have not much to speak of, if anything, as being accomplished through me, for the church to which my life has been given from youth to the present moment. All I can say is I have tried to do something for Christ and the church, as I have opportunity but so far as I know, I am afraid that since I have been in this diocese I have been of little or no use. It is a hard field our Master has called us to labour in."

And so, five years after accepting the call of Christ Church, Scott resigned to enter the U.S. Army as a chaplain. Part of that time he was stationed at Fort Barrancas, and then he went to Mobile, but he visited Pensacola from time to time. He did not remain in the army long and sought other work with the explanation that "while connection with the army was altogether agreeable to me and mine, a sense of duty requires me to place myself in a situation where I might at least hope to be more useful as a clergyman of the church."

In a letter written to Bishop Leonidas Polk, who had ordained him, Scott reflected on his work as a priest: "As to how people like me, how important to some men. I have not yet considered it. I feel an interest in my duties, and in the souls committed to my care, while I try to work upon them to the best advantage. Since I entered the sacred profession, I have never thought of pleasing people, while I have all the while had a great fear of not pleasing Almighty God."

Before leaving for the army, Scott wrote of the need to have an Episcopal bishop spend more time in Pensacola and the need for a church school and college in Pensacola. In 1851, two years before leaving Christ Church, the Rev. Francis Huger Rutledge, a friend of Scott's, was elected the first Bishop of Florida with Scott missing the election by a single vote. Rutledge had been rector of Trinity Church in St. Augustine between the years 1840 and 1845. When elected bishop, he was rector of St. John's in Tallahassee. After the election, Scott wrote that he had no desire to be a bishop though he would not decline if it were God's will. He also added that he would rather be a parish priest because of his love of home and family and the time to study and write. He was relieved "by sincere feelings of gratitude" that God had not called him to a higher and more difficult office in the church.

Among the difficulties Scott faced in Pensacola prior to his entering the army as a chaplain were the extreme Protestantism and congregationalism of the parish. He was also troubled by his salary as is evidenced by his annual report to the diocese in 1849: "The rector's salary is only half enough to live on, and this should be remedied, not for ourselves, but for the honor of the church, and for the glory of God."

After Scott's resignation, the parish continued to be plagued with problems, especially financial ones, and the vestry had difficulty finding a rector. First the vestry called the Rev. N.O. Preston of New Orleans, who declined. Then they called the Rev. David Kerr, who accepted but resigned shortly thereafter. The resignation was sent to the bishop with this interesting note: "Resolved that the letter accompanying the resignation be forwarded to the bishop of the diocese, with a request, that either by its publication, or otherwise we will take measures to protect this parish from the injurious inferences which might be drawn from the unusual circumstances attending the sudden dissolution of the contract between it and our late Rector." There is nothing about this in the parish vestry minutes and nothing in the archives of the Diocese of Florida. The letter was lost. History is silent on this interesting matter.

With David Kerr gone, the vestry called a Rev. Mr. Freeman of Little Rock, Arkansas, who declined. Following that, they called the Rev. David Dubois Flower from Alabama who accepted. Flower, age thirty-one, had founded St. Luke's Church in Jacksonville, Alabama, and then founded St. John's Church in Mobile. He was a graduate of General Theological Seminary in New York City and was ordained to the priesthood by the Rt. Rev. Nicholas Cobbs, Bishop of Alabama, on July 9, 1848. When he arrived in Pensacola, his wife was expecting their first child. After only ten weeks, David Flower died of yellow fever. His son was born the day following his death. His wife died of yellow fever within a few days, and then the infant son died. The parish was devastated. David Flower was buried under the chancel of the church beside the Rev. Frederick Peake and the Rev. Joseph Saunders.

These were difficult and sad years for the parish. On April 17, 1855, the vestry voted to call the Rev. John Jackson Scott of Mobile to return to the rectorship of the parish. On April 23, the following resolution was adopted, "Resolved, that the Rev. J.J. Scott of Mobile be elected rector of this parish, and be respectfully invited to take pastoral charge of the same." Dr. Scott was also asked to take occasional services in Milton.

Why did he return? We can only speculate. Perhaps when he resigned it was because he was discouraged, and his correspondence reflected that. Perhaps he had overextended himself as is evidenced in his request not to continue his work in Warrington. Perhaps it was the salary, and he had told the vestry that because of the low salary the parish ought to have a single man. And maybe it was a problem with churchmanship. Scott was an Anglo-Catholic in a low church diocese. Whatever were the reasons for his leav-

PART TWO, History of Old Christ Church

ing, he was now obviously ready to return, and so he did.

Thus began the second rectorship of Dr. John Jackson Scott, a long rectorship which would span almost the remainder of the nineteenth century, leading the parish through the horrors and devastation of the Civil War and the difficult times of Reconstruction. The parish would grow and flourish under his strong leadership and spiritual direction. He would retire in 1889. Dr. Scott died in 1895 as rector emeritus at the age of eighty.

†

PART THREE

History of Old Christ Church

1855-1867

PART THREE
History of Old Christ Church, 1855-1867

THE GATHERING STORM

HAVING RETURNED TO HIS PARISH IN 1855, DR. SCOTT found the city anxious and fearful over the drift towards secession. Pensacola had grown accustomed to the presence of the military and what that meant to the economy. Also,≠ there was the export trade from the Palafox wharf of cotton and timber. What would happen if there were either secession or war or probably both?

By 1860, Pensacola's population had grown to nearly 3,000, making Pensacola and Key West the two largest cities in the state. In Pensacola both the citizens and the military were preparing for an outright break with the United States. The South had changed since the talk of secession a decade before. Now its economy was stronger and the slavery issue had become paramount due to the dependency of the South upon slave labor. The South now had more shipyards, factories and railroads, and this was especially true in Pensacola.

The election of 1860 turned the tide, and now the storm clouds of war were gathering. Abraham Lincoln was elected President of the United States following a fractured Democratic National Convention in Charleston, South Carolina, when a Southern Democratic party emerged. Because of the fractured Democrats, Lincoln won the election with 180 electoral votes to 123

Palafox Pier, South Palafox Street, 1861. (Courtesy of T.T. Wentworth Jr. Collection, Historic Pensacola Preservation Board)

for his opponents. He had 1,866,452 popular votes against his opponents' combined popular vote of 2,815,617. In the South, Lincoln was called "that black Republican." Time was fast running out.

Shortly after the election of Lincoln, a called convention in South Carolina voted unanimously on December 20, 1860, to approve an ordinance of secession from the Union. Mississippi took similar action on January 9, 1861. Florida followed the next day. On January 11, Alabama joined the states leaving the Union. Then came Georgia on January 19, followed by Louisiana on January 26, and Texas on February 1. On the fourth day of February, delegates from those seven states met in Montgomery, Alabama, to draft a constitution for what they called the Confederate States of

PART THREE, Old Christ Church 1855-1867

America. Jefferson Davis was selected the provisional president and inaugurated on February 18.

FORT SUMTER AND THE WAR BEGINS

Would secession provoke war? When and where would the war begin, and how would it begin? The citizens of Pensacola were forced to take sides. Both Jefferson Davis and Abraham Lincoln were turning their attention to control of government property. Davis and his cabinet were seeking peaceful relations with the government of Lincoln but at the same time were preparing for war. Both Davis and Lincoln were concerned with two forts in particular, Fort Sumter in Charleston harbor and Fort Pickens in Pensacola.

On April 12, 1861, the war started when the Confederates opened fire on Union-held Fort Sumter. Civil War had erupted in the United States. The seven original states of the Confederacy were joined by Virginia, North Carolina, Tennessee and Arkansas.

Meanwhile in Pensacola, the parish of Christ Church held its annual parish meeting on Easter Monday, April 1, 1861. No mention was made in the minutes of the meeting of anything other than the routine elections that took place each year on Easter Monday according to Canon Law. The next recorded vestry minutes were dated December 1866.

Fort Pickens on Santa Rosa Island, across the bay from Pensacola, was formidable for the Confederacy. Union forces at Fort Pickens were strong and would remain so because the Union Navy could reach Fort Pickens by way of the Gulf of Mexico and were out of range of the Southern shore batteries. The South had no navy of any consequence, and so Fort Pickens was reasonably secure. Jefferson Davis received word from Gen. Braxton Bragg, who had just recently assumed command of the Confederate forces in Pensacola, that the prospects for taking the fort by direct assault were not good.

Meanwhile, the Rev. John Jackson Scott met with the general and offered to him whatever services he might perform. General Bragg appointed him a chaplain in the Confederate Army. He was now on active duty but stayed with his family at home while the Confederate forces occupied Pensacola.

Several of Christ Church's parishioners played prominent roles in the Civil War. U.S. Army Col. William Chase was appointed to organize the state militia and was faced with the dilemma of assaulting Union-held Fort Pickens, the structure he built to be invincible. Edward A. Perry rose to the rank of Confederate brigadier general and was assigned to assist with the defense of the city. John Brosnaham, whose family members would be prominent in the parish after the war, was mayor of Pensacola at the time of the city's surrender. Even though the Confederates engaged Fort Pickens

Confederate soldiers at Pensacola Navy Yard. (Courtesy of T.T. Wentworth Jr. Collection, Historic Pensacola Preservation Board)

PART THREE, Old Christ Church 1855-1867

several times, it never fell to them and remained in control of the Union troops throughout the war. Fort Barrancas and Fort McRee were under control of the Confederates until the evacuation of the city.

Meanwhile the Bishop of Louisiana, Leonidas Polk, and the Bishop of Georgia, Stephen Elliott, the senior bishops in the dioceses of the Confederacy, called a special convention to meet in Montgomery on July 3, 1861, to consider establishing the Protestant Episcopal Church in the Confederate States of America. They were careful to keep the Book of Common Prayer and the faith of the church. The prayer for the President of the United States was changed to read for the President of the Confederate States of America. Before that convention met in Montgomery, the annual convention of the Diocese of Florida met in Jacksonville at St. John's Church with John J. Scott as a clerical delegate. Approving the called convention in Montgomery, they elected Scott as a clerical delegate to that convention. The convention in Montgomery approved the establishment of the Protestant Episcopal Church in the Confederate States of America, but the Diocese of Florida did not ratify the constitution of the Confederate Church until December 1863.

Back in Pensacola the conflict grew. St. John's Church in Warrington, only recently completed, was struck by a shell during the first bombardment of November 22, 1861. It burned to the ground. By the spring of 1862, Confederate forces evacuated Jacksonville and St. Augustine. In February of that year, General Bragg was ordered to leave Pensacola and go as quickly as possible to Tennessee by way of Mississippi, where his army would meet with the army of General Johnston for what would become the famous Battle of Shiloh.

Bragg gave orders to torch the city as the Confederates left, destroying as quickly as they could anything that would be of value to the enemy. The economy of Pensacola was gone. The mills were burned. Railroad tracks were destroyed as Bragg's army left. Fort Barrancas, Fort McRee, and the Navy Yard went up in smoke. Almost everyone left the city. Some fled to Greenville, Alabama, but Dr. Scott and most of his parishioners went to Montgomery, Alabama. The Union troops moved in and confiscated everything they could use including Stephen Mallory's house on Palafox Street, which became the new home of Col. William Wilson. By July 1863, Dr. John Brosnaham, who chose to remain in Pensacola, wrote that all the citizens had left except for seventy-two white people and ten blacks.

In Montgomery, with his "parish in exile," Dr. Scott continued his priesthood ministering to those who had come with him to that city as well as those who turned to him in need. He was still a chaplain in the Confederate Army, and so he ministered to the military stationed in Montgomery. He kept a parish register of weddings, funerals, and baptisms while there, as well as some notes on the formation of the Church of the Holy Comforter. At first Scott wanted to name the new church in memory of the late Bishop of Alabama, the Rt. Rev. Nicholas H. Cobbs, who had died in 1861, but the rector of St. John's did not like the idea. It is interesting to note that the rector of St. John's was the son-in-law of Bishop Cobbs. Dr. Scott wrote his disappointment and added that the rector of St. John's Church "claimed in some sense and manner to represent Bishop Cobbs' memory." The Bishop of Alabama, Richard Wilmer, suggested that it be named Holy Comforter.

The new church in Montgomery was housed in the former Universalist Church on the corner of Perry and South Alabama Street. In the Parish Register, Dr. Scott writes: "The Church or Parish was commenced and founded by the Rev. J. Jackson Scott, S.T.D., Priest of the Diocese of Florida, driven from his Parish in Pensacola at the evacuation of that city by the Confederate forces and the entrance into it by the Federal Army..."

During the occupation of Pensacola, Christ Church became in turn a barracks, jail, hospital, and finally a military chapel established by a chaplain in the United States Army who was in priest's orders. The church building was badly damaged and desecrated. Many of the furnishings in the church building were destroyed along with the organ. Dr. Scott's house was burned. The school building was damaged by fire. The school had been founded during Dr. Scott's early years at Christ Church and in 1858 had two full-time teachers as well as the rector.

PART THREE, Old Christ Church 1855-1867

THE EXILES RETURN

Pensacola natives began to return to their devastated city in 1864, then in greater numbers after Lee's surrender at Appomattox on April 9, 1865. The Confederacy came to an end in Florida when Union troops moved into Tallahassee on May 20 of that same year. A month earlier, the Union army had entered Greenville, Alabama, and Pensacola's exiled government ended. When those who had evacuated the city for refuge in Greenville and Montgomery finally came home, they found little of what they had left. Businesses were destroyed. Homes had been sacked and burned. Refugees were living in shacks near Fort Barrancas, and some had taken refuge in the Christ Church school.

Just as Bragg's Confederate Army had burned and destroyed everything they could when they left, so did the Union Army destroy what it could when it moved out of the city. Almost everything was gone. Fortunes were lost. Businesses were bankrupt. Much of Palafox Street was in ruins. Many were homeless. But Christ Church was still standing. It was there as a beacon of hope for the community.

With the war ended, it was time now to recover from the ravages of war and to begin again, to rebuild their city and their church. Even though Dr. Scott had been the one to make the motion in Diocesan Convention that the Diocese of Florida unite with the Protestant Episcopal Church in the Confederate States of America, he supported the move by the General Convention of the Church in October 1865 to bring the Southern churches back into the Protestant Episcopal Church in the United States of America. Bishop Rutledge of Florida, along with the Episcopal bishops of North Carolina, Tennessee, and Arkansas, all took their seats in the House of Bishops. At the Diocesan Council in 1866, Bishop Rutledge presiding, the Council voted to unite with the Protestant Episcopal Church in the United States of America. The schism was over. The church was again united. And the Episcopal Church avoided the divisions that continued in other churches well into the twentieth century.

Venerable old Bishop Rutledge, frail and weak from the war and the trials and tribulations of those terrible days, died on November 5, 1866, in Tallahassee. He had been confined to his bed for several months. Not long before death came to him, he asked to be taken to St. John's Church, where he had served as rector and where his office as bishop had been located, so he could receive the Holy Communion with his people. Funeral services were held at St. John's Church in Tallahassee, and he was buried in the cemetery of the Church of the Holy Cross in Stateburg, South Carolina.

And so, when John Jackson Scott and his flock of Christ Church returned to Pensacola, not only was the city almost destroyed, but their beloved bishop also had died. When did Dr. Scott return? We do not know. But we do know that the first recorded vestry minutes following the war are dated December 1866. In the minute book, it is as if nothing had happened between April 1, 1861, and December 1866. In the minutes of the vestry, one turns the page, and five years are as if they had never been.

The leaders of the parish prior to the war assumed their responsibilities and leadership after the war. Between 1859 and 1861 are the names of W.H. Chase, Henry Hyer, A.C. Blount, A.L. Avery, W.E. Anderson, C.C. Yonge, W.H. Judah, Louis Hyer, and Walker Anderson. Present at the first vestry meeting in 1866 were A.C. Blount, A.E. Maxwell and Louis Hyer, the son of Henry Hyer, who died in 1867. The next year W.E. Anderson and A.L. Avery are back on the vestry. Had they all been in Montgomery with Dr. Scott? We do not know. But this we do know. As soon as the exiles returned to the city, they picked up the pieces and started over again.

In 1861, the population of Florida was 140,000, and Florida was the least populous state in the Confederate States of America with almost one half of that population being either free blacks or slaves. In West Florida, one half of all the citizens resided in Santa Rosa and Escambia counties, comprising about fifteen percent of the population of Florida but with only eight percent of the slaves in the state.

The first action of the vestry at its December 1866 meeting was to elect a vestryman to fill the vacancy occasioned by the death of W.H. Baker and

PART THREE, Old Christ Church 1855-1867

to elect delegates to represent the parish at the Diocesan Council to be held in Tallahassee the following year. By May 27, 1867, the vestry was concerned with "the expense of putting the church in a condition to ensure its preservation," determining "at what cost the church can be repaired inside and out" and reporting on "matters touching on the restoration of the church to its condition prior to the late war."

In his report to the Diocese of Florida, Dr. Scott wrote of the desecration of the church building during the war. In that same report he wrote of the destruction of St. John's, Warrington, as well as his own home and major damage to the parish school building. The organ in the church had been destroyed. A portion of the floor of the chancel had been removed, and the coffins of two of the former rectors buried under the floor had been exposed and desecrated by Union soldiers. It was later reported that George Hallmark, a young man at the time of the occupation of the city, saw the Union soldiers dig up the graves while he was a prisoner confined to the church building.

George Hallmark, we learn from the Parish Register of Christ Church, was born in 1846, confirmed in 1870 at St. John's Church in Warrington by Bishop John Freeman Young, and served on the vestry of Christ Church from 1878 to 1888 and again from 1890 to 1900. He died July 12, 1906, at the age of sixty and was buried two days later at St. John's Cemetery. His daughter, Daisy Hallmark, passed on the story of young George as a prisoner during the Civil War.

Other members of the vestry prior to the Civil War who continued to serve the parish after the war deserve mention. Walker Anderson, who served the parish for many years and was involved in diocesan matters, was also a leader in the growth of the city during those years. He was chief justice of the Supreme Court of Florida and was elected the first lay delegate to the General Convention of the Church from the Diocese of Florida. Following in his father's footsteps was William Edward Anderson, who was at one time mayor of the city. He was a longtime vestryman, secretary of the vestry, superintendent of the Sunday School and lay reader. He died in 1908. His son, Walker Anderson, was also active in the life of the parish. He died in 1920.

Albert L. Avery was on the vestry before and after the Civil War. Alexander Clement Blount, on the vestry prior to the war, was a colonel in the Confederate Engineers. He came to the city in 1859 and took his place in the leadership of both city and parish. He was the father of three other parish and city leaders: Frederick N. Blount, William Alexander Blount, and A.C. Blount Jr. Henry Hyer was a leader in the life of Christ Church prior to the war, and his son, Louis Hyer, was on the vestry after the exiles returned to the city. Another son, William Kopman Hyer, born in 1836, served with distinction in the Civil War, retiring at the end of the war as a captain. He died in 1913 after having served both the parish and the city. He was senior warden of the parish for many years, a city alderman, and a member of the state legislature.

William H. Judah, a pioneer in the lumber business both before and after the war, established Keyser Judah and Company, which after the war became one of the leading export businesses in Northwest Florida. He served on the vestry before and after the war and died in 1878. A.E. Maxwell was on the vestry by the time of the 1866 meeting and continued to serve the parish for many years to come. Over the years, Judge Maxwell held numerous positions of great importance in the state, was a senator from Florida in the Confederate States of America, later served as a state senator, and was one of the most eminent jurists in the state.

Another outstanding leader both in the parish and the city was Edward Alysworth Perry, born in 1833, who came to Pensacola as a young man to practice law. He was a vestryman of Christ Church for many years. Perry was a colonel in the 2nd Florida Regiment and in 1862 was made brigadier general. He distinguished himself in the Battle of Seven Pines, the Seven Days' Battle near Richmond, as well as at Gettysburg. He was elected governor of Florida in 1884.

Other prominent Pensacola citizens who served on the vestry during the difficult days of Reconstruction include Benjamin Drake Wright, who was a member of the Territorial Legislature, United States district attorney, chief justice of the state supreme court as well as editor of the *Pensacola Gazette*. Chandler Cox Yonge was active for many years in Christ Church,

PART THREE, Old Christ Church 1855-1867

moving to Pensacola in 1859. He was the father of Philip K. Yonge and Chandler C. Yonge Jr., both of whom were active members of the parish.

Immediately following the return of Dr. Scott and the members of the parish, it was necessary to secure the building, make immediate repairs, and begin plans for a new school building. The Rev. Frederick Peake had started the school in 1845, and it had continued under the leadership of Dr. Scott prior to the war. By the 1880s the school was the largest parochial educational institution in the diocese, and the school building was valued at $2,500, according to the Diocesan Journal of 1883.

But in 1867 the school building was in shambles, and there was little money available for reconstruction. Dr. Scott appealed to the vestry for help, reminding them that for several years the school had been in his home and that he and his wife were the only teachers. He also reminded the vestry that he had never asked for any money to run the school and had relied on donations from those both within and outside the parish. Now he wanted to establish the Parish School of Christ Church and needed a school building since the one on Church Street had been all but destroyed. He would serve as rector of the school, and it would fall under the authority of the canons of the diocese. He also wanted the school to be open to any child. Even though it would be necessary to charge a fee, he wanted all those who could not afford it to be able to attend free. He also reminded the vestry that three years after his coming to Christ Church, the school moved to a building of its own. Mrs. E. Cozzens had both taught and run the school, which had grown considerably by the time of the evacuation of the city.

When Dr. Scott returned after the war, the school building was being used as a shelter for the poor and repairs were under way to make it habitable. Dr. Scott further reported in 1867 that a gift had been made to him as "a Christmas offering for the Rector," and he had used it to improve the building and to buy school furniture. In this report, he concluded that the parishioners needed to "put their hand to the plough and to help the work by donations, influence, and sending of children."

"The Parish School, as little as it became after so many years, has been in my care all through those eventful years, and it is considered by me so important an agency for propagation of Christ's true religion that I hardly know a higher honor next to the planting of a church than that of founding a Parish School," Dr. Scott wrote the vestry. With the building under repair, he stated that there were accommodations for only twenty-five, but that he would like the building enlarged to accommodate at least one hundred pupils and additional teachers.

The vestry approved Dr. Scott's plan for making the school a parochial school under the direction of the rector and with the support of the vestry. The vestry further authorized that the property be transferred to the rector, wardens, and vestry of Christ's Church in Pensacola.

Now it was time for the parish to turn its attention to repairs to the church and to possible enlargement of the building.

PART FOUR

History of Old Christ Church

1867-1997

PART FOUR
History of Old Christ Church, 1867-1997

THE DAWNING OF A NEW AGE

WHEN THE WAR WAS OVER, PENSACOLA RESIDENTS REturned to their devastated city, and they began to rebuild. And rebuild they did. It was slow at first. The vestry of Christ Church had few resources, but they made the necessary temporary repairs to the church building and the school house. In 1867 conditions were better, and the vestry asked A.C. Blount and A.L. Avery to "ascertain at what cost the church can be repaired inside and out, and to include in the report to be submitted by them on matters touching the restoration of the church to its condition prior to the late war." The vestry also became more assertive in encouraging the congregation to give more money for the church and the school.

By 1870, Pensacola was a different place. The population was growing. At this same time, the railroad to Montgomery was built, roads were under construction, mills were reopened, and new businesses were developed. And there was something new in the city—the Pensacola Telegraph Company, which linked the city to points north, west, and east. Business was coming to town.

Col. William H. Chase died in 1870, but his railroad became a reality with the establishment of the Pensacola & Louisville Railroad. Chase had not returned to the vestry after the war, obviously busy fulfilling his dream for a railroad and the restoration of his city.

And at this same time, the Pensacola port was expanding with a new industry, the export of yellow pine, which would give Pensacola a boom economy for the next decades. The harbor, combined with this new business, became the economic basis for the dawning of a new age. During the post-Civil War years, attention was also turned to the development of the Navy Yard, which had been shut down during the war.

A.C. Blount, W.K. Hyer, W.H. Judah, W.F. Lee, and C.C. Yonge were some of those who revitalized both the city and the church. A.C. Blount was interested in the development of the downtown. W.K. Hyer rebuilt his ship brokerage company. W.H. Judah developed the timber business. W.F.

Palafox Street, 1875. (Courtesy of Christ Church Archives)

PART FOUR, Old Christ Church 1867-1997

Lee worked in civil engineering and served as postmaster. C.C. Yonge, the father of Philip K. Yonge and Chandler C. Yonge Jr., not only practiced law, but also was involved in the financial development of the city. Philip and Chandler later became prominent leaders in the parish and in the city. And in 1872, Henry Baars came to Pensacola and Christ Church. The Baars family would remain active in the life of Christ Church for generations to come.

And so by 1877, the time had come for Christ Church to begin making plans either for the relocation of the church or for major renovations and improvements to the present church structure. At the vestry meeting of September 1877, it was decided that the rector, Dr. Scott, be authorized to "communicate with the Bishop of the Diocese, the Rt. Rev. J.F. Young, in regard to the proposed changes to the church and to request the bishop to have plans and specifications drawn out by an experienced ecclesiastical architect." By January 1878, Dr. Scott presented plans and specifications from Charles C. Haight, an architect from New York City. A.L. Avery was appointed to request estimates from various builders in the city.

In April of that year, Bishop Young visited the parish and attended the vestry meeting to discuss the plans under way for the expansion of the church building. A.L. Avery asked the vestry to approve the purchase, not exceeding nine dollars per thousand, of about 50,000 bricks, which were then on sale in the city, and to have these bricks "hauled up to the church lot." Mr. Haight's bill was $150.

However, in 1879, the vestry was having trouble paying the sexton. He had not been paid for seventeen months and was owed $200. The secretary was asked to call upon the members of the parish in an attempt to collect the money. The vestry was also having trouble paying the Diocesan Assessment. In June, the subject of constructing a new church was discussed but it was decided the parish did not have the means to do that. Then the vestry passed the following resolution: "That Mr. Areson be requested to prepare and submit an estimate with detailed specifications for the extension of the church twenty feet in a westerly direction, for raising the tower and putting on a new roof in accordance with the plans prepared by Mr. Chas. C. Haight of New York. . ."

54 THE SEARCH FOR THE LOST RECTORS

Two days later the vestry met with Joseph Areson, who submitted an estimate "to extend the church twenty feet in a westerly direction, to make a new roof and do all repairs and improvements in accordance with plans and specifications submitted for the sum of $4,500.00." The proposal was accepted. A committee of two members, W.E. Anderson and W.K. Hyer, were appointed to act as supervisors of the construction and to inspect and

Interior of Old Christ Church after the installation of the stained glass windows in 1884. Central window over the altar was installed in 1879 as a memorial to the Rt. Rev. Francis Huger Rutledge, First Bishop of Florida. (Courtesy of Christ Archives)

PART FOUR, Old Christ Church 1867-1997

approve all material and "to do whatever is necessary to ensure a faithful compliance with conditions of contract." The members of the vestry were C.C. Yonge, A.L. Avery, W.H. Judah, W.E. Anderson, and W.K. Hyer Jr., leading citizens of the dawning of a new age in church and city.

In his report to the Diocese of Florida for the year 1879, Dr. Scott reported that "a handsome stained-glass chancel window has been erected as a memorial to the late Bishop Rutledge." This "Light of the World" window was the first stained-glass window placed in Christ Church. In June 1884, the vestry authorized the rector to order additional stained-glass windows from Edward Colegate of New York, one of the leading manufacturers of stained-glass in America. Fourteen windows were ordered at $100 each, two small windows at $50 each, and a memorial window at $200. The memorial window, the "Woman of Samaria," was given by the Hyer family with the inscription: "To the Glory of God And In Loving Memory of Henry, Born September 13th, 1792, Died December 14th, 1868, And, Julia Hyer, Born December 13th, 1796, Died April 13th, 1858." The other windows were neo-Gothic and geometric in design, typical of the style of the nineteenth century. The Hyer memorial window and the Rutledge memorial window were moved from Christ Church to the new Christ Church in 1903 along with five of the other neo-Gothic geometric-style windows, which are reputed to be some of the finest examples of stained-glass windows in America from the nineteenth century.

That same year Dr. Scott reported to the vestry that he had received $750 from the insurance company for the school destroyed by fire. The vestry asked him to submit a plan for rebuilding the school building. On March 6, 1885, A.V. Clubbs submitted a bid to rebuild the school on Church Street for $923. The Bishop of Florida, John Freeman Young, died later that year, and a new bishop, Edwin G. Weed, was elected the following year.

As the parish grew, an assistant for Dr. Scott, who was now in his seventies, was added to the staff. At the July 6, 1886, meeting of the vestry it was announced that the Ladies Aid Society had offered to donate a pipe organ to the parish to be built by Messers G.H. Ryder & Company of Boston. In September, the vestry authorized a committee to contract for the construction of an organ chamber "same to be of proper size to hold the new organ, to be of good hard brick and covered with a tin roof with felt underneath." On April 13, 1887, the vestry was informed that the total cost of the new organ installed would be $1,907.66.

That October, Dr. Scott told the vestry he had talked with Bishop Weed about his desire to have a missionary come to Pensacola to work with the "colored people" in the community. Zion Chapel, which he had established shortly after the war, had grown, and Dr. Scott felt it would be beneficial to have a priest here for that work as well as to assist him with "such other duties as may be required of him." The vestry supported the rector and pledged to raise $600 towards the salary of the missionary.

And then the time had come. April 21, 1889, Easter Sunday, was Dr. Scott's last Easter as rector of Christ Church. He had seen the parish grow from a small number of communicants to one of the largest and strongest in the Diocese of Florida. He had led the parish through the difficult years prior to the Civil War. He had taken the exiles to Montgomery. He had brought his flock back to a devastated city and a desecrated church building. He had led the parish through the hardships of Reconstruction. He had seen the church building he loved so dearly expanded and refurbished. Now, at age seventy-four, it was time for him to retire.

The following letter from the Rector's Desk was sent to the vestrymen of Christ Church Parish, P.K. Yonge, Senior Warden, and W.K. Hyer, Junior Warden: "Gentlemen: It is with some degree of reluctance I address you, but I am constrained to do so, from circumstances that I think I ought to allow to govern my actions. It is known to you, as to others, that I have devoted my life to the service of Christ and his Church, and that without intermission, as I have never sought what is known among clergymen as a vacation. But now, with the appearance of a high state of health, I feel at times much prostration, accompanied by mental depression, to which I have never been accustomed. There are causes for this, to which I desire not to give expression. I only seek a relief for this condition of my physical and mental system, which I hope to find in a change of climate and associations and relaxation for a few months.

PART FOUR, Old Christ Church 1867-1997

"I have been returned as a deputy in the General Convention to meet in New York about the first of October. Now what I desire is to give myself an opportunity of rest so as to be in my place at the convention at its opening. I cannot ask your sanction of my absence for the time specified, as it may materially affect the interest and welfare of the parish, which I consider of more importance than my health. I must ask you therefore to accept my resignation as Rector of Christ Church.

"This is the alternative which affects me seriously and painfully, as I have been ministering to you and your fathers for, by far, the larger part of my life, and many and tender have been the associations that have sprung up and wound themselves about my heart and being, as tendrils of a plant nourished for good, and though blighted by perils and often prostrated and seemingly dead for awhile, yet still live on, showing signs of greenness and an undying life, that will flourish in more perfect form and beauty amid the unchanging issues of our Father's Kingdom beyond the Stars, with Christ and his redeemed ones. To say nothing of my efforts, sacrifices, and labors that I have found myself able to make and do with his Grace helping and sustaining me in many a weary day, for the record has gone before; and is out of the reach of ingratitude and vituparation, and I am the sole and only one who must answer to my Master, Christ, in the day of solemn judgment. I claim no merit to myself, but only trust that what I have done to the best of my poor ability will be accepted, because washed and cleansed with His most precious blood, and though my work may fail, I may be saved yet, so as by fire, through our most holy and merciful Savior, in whom I live and move and have my being.

"I commend you and our church to God and the riches of his grace, who will not fail the humble and contrite who lean trustingly on Him. Wherever my lot may be cast, and whatever may betide me in my earthly pilgrimage, I shall not cease to remember you when I pray for myself before the throne of Grace as a poor trembling sinner, who looks to be saved by that same grace that lifted the dying penitent from the Cross and placed him securely in Paradise."

On May 23, 1889, at a special meeting of the vestry the communication from Dr. Scott was presented. The vestry accepted the resignation and offered him a leave of absence from June 1 to November 1 with his salary continuing during that time. The vestry also unanimously elected him rector emeritus at a salary of $1,000 per year.

Then the vestry unanimously adopted the following resolution: "Whereas our Rector, the Rev. Dr. J.J. Scott has resigned the rectorship of this parish, and the vestry believing that the same was done after careful consideration, and having full confidence in his mature judgment, have accepted the same. Therefore, be it resolved, that we, the wardens and vestry of Christ Church Parish, desire to place on record our appreciation of the earnest life and lofty character of our beloved rector; that we hereby express our grateful recognition of his long and faithful services in this parish; and our unfeigned admiration of his service of devotion to duty. And it is with the deepest regret that we are called upon to sever our connection that has existed between him and this parish for the past thirty-nine years, and that though

Looking east from corner of Palafox and Government Streets, 1896 with Pensacola Opera House on the right. (Courtesy of T.T. Wentworth Jr. Collection, Historic Pensacola Preservation Board)

PART FOUR, Old Christ Church 1867-1997

the outward bonds are severed, the tender ties of love and devotion, which bind us and his congregation to him, can never be broken, that we earnestly trust he will remain in our midst, where we may, as of old, go to him as a dear friend in our trials and troubles. . ."

Dr. Scott responded with a letter of appreciation and concluded: "My hope is that rest and diversion will relieve the strain on my nervous system and restore me to that condition in which I may be able to work again with satisfaction to myself and with some degree of benefit to the church and the souls of my fellow creatures before I go hence and be no more seen."

Between August 1889 and April 1890, the vestry called seven priests, each of whom declined the call. On March 26, 1890, Bishop Weed recommended a priest from Summerville, South Carolina, the Rev. Percival Hanahan Whaley, age thirty-seven. Born on Edisto Island, South Carolina in 1853, he graduated from Porter Military Academy in Charleston, South Carolina; Trinity College in Hartford, Connecticut; and Berkley Divinity School at Yale University in New Haven, Connecticut.

Mr. Whaley was destined to lead the parish out of the nineteenth century and into the twentieth century. Dr. Scott continued to assist the parish when his health permitted. He died on November 21, 1895, in this eightieth year. He was buried from his parish church beside his wife's mother in St. John's Cemetery in Pensacola.

The following is part of a resolution adopted by the vestry at a special meeting on November 30, 1895: "With sympathy and prayer and words of pious consolation, as well as active effort to relieve suffering, he faithfully fulfilled the duties of the loving man, as well as the Christian Priest. Prompt and fearless in his condemnation of wrong, but tender and pitiful to those who were penitent, his people learned to trust with entire faith his justice and his sympathy. Those in trouble went to him for advice, those in doubt for consolation, those in distress for comfort, and his large heart gave to all as they needed. The oldest priest in the Diocese, both in years and in Canonical Residence, a profound scholar and theologian, his death creates a loss to the Diocese and to the church, as well as to this Parish. . ."

The Rev. John Jackson Scott had served the parish and the church at large with great distinction. He barely missed being elected Bishop of Florida twice—the first time when Francis Huger Rutledge was elected First Bishop of Florida, and the second time, following Bishop Rutledge's death when John Freeman Young was elected Second Bishop of Florida. Both times he had the clergy votes but lacked enough lay votes to be elected.

During his years in Pensacola, Dr. Scott served the Diocese of Florida in

The Rev. Percival Hanahan Whaley, rector from 1890 to 1908. (Courtesy of Christ Church Archives)

PART FOUR, Old Christ Church 1867-1997

every important position, including archdeacon, dean of the Western Convocation, examining chaplain, and president of the Standing Committee and the Board of Missions. He was a clerical deputy to General Convention fifteen times, the most of any priest at that time. He was a member of the first Board of Trustees of the University of the South and was responsible for the establishment of St. John's Church, Warrington; St. Mary's Church, Milton; Zion Chapel; and St. Cyprian's; and a mission church at Bluff Springs.

During Percival Whaley's early years as rector of Christ Church, relocating the church was discussed from time to time. The Seville Square area was deteriorating, and families were moving into the new North Hill and East Hill areas. Then on June 19, 1899, Mr. Whaley called a meeting of the vestry to consider the "expediency of purchasing the property of the Bell estate on the corner of Wright and Palafox Streets." Mr. Whaley also informed the vestry that the Ladies Society had authorized an additional loan of $1,200 against the rectory property if necessary to make the cash payment on the purchase. The vestry approved the purchase, and plans were now underway for a new church building. In August, the vestry sold the school building and lot, the proceeds to be used for the construction of the new church.

And on that note, working and planning for the future, the nineteenth century came to an end.

By the spring of 1900, $15,775 had been pledged toward the construction of a new church building. Throughout that year and into the next, the vestry continued trying to raise the necessary funds. In March 1901 the vestry began consultations with John Sutcliffe, an architect from Chicago. In August, Mr. Sutcliffe was retained and asked to prepare plans and specifications for a building not to exceed $25,000.

In February 1902, A.D. Alfred's bid for construction of the building was approved at a cost of $24,475. In March 1902, the vestry was making plans to have some of the stained-glass windows moved from the old church to the new church along with the memorial plaques to the former rectors, the altar rail, the altar, and other church furnishings. The cornerstone of the new building was laid on June 4, 1902, and the building was finished in 1903. The last service in the old church was Good Friday 1903, and the first service in the new church was on Easter Sunday. The old had passed away; the new had come.

OLD CHRIST CHURCH IN THE TWENTIETH CENTURY

When the congregation of Christ Church, Seville Square, moved to the new church building on the corner of Wright and Palafox streets, the old church building was used by St. Cyprian's Episcopal Church until 1928. St. Cyprian's had been organized by the Rev. John Jackson Scott, and under the direction of the Rev. Percival Whaley, it became an official mission of the Diocese of Florida. It was named St. Cyprian's after the Bishop of Carthage in the third century. It may have been the successor of Zion Chapel, an earlier African-American mission established by Dr. Scott.

Some of the furnishings of the old building were moved to the new Christ Church in 1903. The stained-glass window, "The Light of the World," a memorial to the first Bishop of Florida, was dedicated to Bishop Rutledge. Originally installed in 1879, it was moved to the west transcept of the new church building along with five of the neo-Gothic geometric stained-glass windows, three in the nave and two in the narthex. The "Woman of Samaria" window, a memorial to Henry and Julia Hyer, was placed in the east nave.

Other memorials moved from the old church to the new church included the memorial tablets for Joseph Hubbard Saunders, Frederick Foote Peake, David Dubois Flower and John Jackson Scott; the west and east altar rails in memory of Eben Walker Dorr and Louis Hyer; brass altar vases; the altar cross in memory of Josephine Hyer Knowles; the litany desk in memory of Edna Browning Blocker; the large wooden eagle lectern in memory of Mary Walthall Dorr Roberts; the credence table in memory of J.C. and C.R. Whiting; two hymn boards in memory of Josephine Loring Knowles; the baptismal font in memory of John E. Davis and Sarah C.

PART FOUR, Old Christ Church 1867-1997

The Rev. Percival Whaley, rector, (top row) with acolytes and the boys' choir at north entrance to Old Christ Church. Whaley became rector in 1890. The congregation moved to the present church in 1903. (Courtesy of Christ Church Archives)

Davis; a bronze tablet in memory of John A. Cameron, the author of the Constitution and Canons of the Diocese of Florida; and two silver and gold chalices, two silver and gold patens, and a silver alms basin bought by Dr. Scott in 1851. Also brought from the old church were a reading desk and priest's chair. The original altar was loaned to St. Paul's Church, Quincy, Florida, and was returned to Christ Church several years ago.

Between the time St. Cyprian's Church left old Christ Church in 1928 to move into its own building and 1936, when the vestry of Christ Church deeded the building to the city, it was empty and fell victim to vandals. The pews disappeared. The windows were broken out. The roof leaked.

From the "Personal Recollections Of Old Christ Church" by Miss Lelia Abercrombie, we find a wealth of information about the years prior to 1936. Miss Abercrombie reports that in 1929 "a firm desiring to buy the property and use Old Christ Church for a warehouse approached the vestry with their proposal; however, Mr. Frank Milner and Mr. Ashton Brosnaham prevented it from being accepted." It had been spared the ravages of the Civil War. In 1879 it was again spared when the congregation decided to remain at Seville Square and enlarge the building rather than build a new church. And then once more in 1929, with Miss Lelia Abercrombie's determination, the building was saved.

Miss Abercrombie continues her story. "The building and its fate continued to be a topic of much discussion in the parish. Somehow the matter could never be settled satisfactorily. One evening when Mr. and Mrs. H.G. DeSilva, Miss Emily Coit, Mr. W.W. White, and I were visiting together in the living room at 110 West Gadsden Street, the subject came up. A few remarks were made to the effect that it would be a good thing if the building would just burn down or blow away or be demolished! I got madder and madder for I had always loved the atmosphere of peace and beauty, the muted tones of the lovely wood. Miss Louise (Yonge) had taught us that the roof built in the shape of an inverted ship's hull was symbolical of the apostles being fishermen. Finally I stomped out of the room with the remark, 'If I ever have a penny I shall restore it!' When I calmed down I returned. The subject had been dropped, but a few years later I received an inheritance from a second cousin-in-law. I remembered my vow. When I visited Dr. Hendree Harrison, rector of Christ Church, and told him my desire, he tried to discourage me, reminding me that we were in a deep depression (it was 1933); and the money could well have been spent to feed the hungry, but I was determined. When my sister, S. Cary Abercrombie, came on a visit from Washington in March, I told her my plans; she said she wanted to have perpetual care taken of our cemetery lot in St. John's, and the one in St. Michael's cemented over. We decided to pool our resources and do several things in which we were both interested.

"Dr. Harrison cooperated beautifully. Having been a civil engineer, he knew exactly how to go about measuring, buying, and planning, and with the help of ordinary carpenters, the repairs were made. Because of the beauty and historic interest of the building, the city permitted a cypress shingle

PART FOUR, Old Christ Church 1867-1997

roof to be put on. An ordinance required that a composition roof be used ordinarily, because of the fire hazard entailed by wood.

"The beams were sagging, the roof leaking and many of the windows were broken. The city was on the verge of condemning the building. It was being damaged constantly by vandals. Marjorie Yonge attempted to raise money to help with the project but only succeeded in securing $22.50. The money was used to buy a marble plaque, which was designed by Dr. Harrison and placed at the right of the front door. The marble had a flaw in it and cost less than usual.

"One lovely day in the spring of 1936, I had an urge to visit the beautiful old building on my lunch hour; much to my dismay, I found many windows again broken. I circled the square and went to the office of Mr. Roark, who was city manager at the time. I was very fond of Mr. Roark, he had been most cooperative through the years when I was doing the St. Nicholas Girls work. I told him what I had found and added, 'Can't you give the old building special police protection; you know, I am Scottish and don't like to see my money wasted!' He replied that he could not give special police protection unless the city owned the building; but, 'If you can get the church to deed the property to the city, we would love to use it for a public library.'"

On April 3, 1936, the city manager responded with a letter to the effect that if the vestry of Christ Church would deed the old church to the city, the property would be accepted for use as a public library and museum, that the building would be maintained by the city, and "upon failure of the city for any calender year to keep the property in a well-repaired state that it shall revert to the grantors." This agreement also stipulated that the grounds would be maintained and landscaped by the City of Pensacola.

In her "Recollections," Miss Abercrombie tells the end of the story of the transfer of Old Christ Church to the City of Pensacola. "Easter was only a few weeks away and I knew that Bishop Juhan would be in Pensacola on that day, so I wrote him and his wife, asking them to have supper with me that evening. We were without a minister, Dr. Harrison having passed away in January 1936. I also asked Hal A. Brosnaham, senior warden of

66 THE SEARCH FOR THE LOST RECTORS

Christ Church, and his wife; Miss Emily Coit; and Mr. W.W. White to the supper. I presented my cause to the bishop and 'Cousin Hal,' and they agreed to give the matter serious consideration. I later presented the case to each member of the vestry. The subject failed to be brought up at the following meeting as had been promised so the morning of the next vestry meeting each vestryman received a copy of the letter. . . stating the city's suggestions.

"As the old building had been the center of much controversy, it was urgent that the transaction be completed before the arrival of the new minister, so that he might not have the burden of this question to cloud the days of his ministry at Christ Church from the very beginning. I felt that, if the matter were settled before his arrival, his road would be a bit smoother. At the time I did not know it would be Dr. Henry Bell Hodgkins, who has since served so many years in Pensacola. The bishop came over the summer of 1936 and deconsecrated the building. On August 28, 1936, the deed, which had been drawn up by Judge E. C. Maxwell, was signed by the following vestrymen:

H.A. Brosnaham, senior warden
Norborne A. Brown, junior warden
W.C. Currie
W.W. White
G.D. Hallmark
R.B. Morrison
Lovett Keyser

"Old Christ Church was turned over to the city for the sum of $1. W.P.A. workers immediately got to work converting the building into a library."

Old Christ Church continued to be used as the first public library in Pensacola until 1959 when it had outgrown the space and moved into a larger building. The old church was then turned over to the Pensacola Historical Society for use as a museum and historical archives.

PART FOUR, Old Christ Church 1867-1997

THE RETURN OF OLD CHRIST CHURCH
TO ITS ORIGINAL OWNER

I first visited Old Christ Church in February 1966 and met with Miss Abercrombie, the first of many such visits. She was one of my parishioners, and I was eager to learn more about the history of the parish of which I had just become rector. Miss Abercrombie was born in 1892 and was baptized at Old Christ Church. She remembered a lot about her early years attending services in the old church. She told me she still remembered catching the horse-drawn streetcar at Gregory and Palafox streets and later, when older, being able to walk from 202 East Jackson Street to church. In her "Recollections," she wrote about Sunday services. "The Hyer and Whiting families sat on the front pew of the center aisle. The Hyer twins were present at most of the services. Miss Sallie Ann and Miss Julia Ann were short and fat and just waddled down the aisle. The Baars were never on time, arriving as a rule after the reading of the first lesson. Of course, there were the Yonge family, the J.C. Averys, Minor Avery, Willis and Walker Anderson, the Beards (twins also), Morenos, Bells, Ingrahams, W.H. Knowles, W.D. Keysers, Brosnahams. We sat in the back row, middle aisle, to the left. Seats were arranged with double pews down the center and an aisle on each side; then there were pews by the windows. The side pews went to the front windows but the center pews were about ten feet from the front door. Lamps were on the side walls and branch holders down the center on the partition dividing the pews. There was a potbellied stove to warm the building. It was located to the right just west of the first north window."

It was difficult for me to imagine the interior of the building because in 1966 it was filled with antiques and tables for research and work in the chancel. Even then, the building was not in very good repair. It was showing its age and lack of maintenance.

Over the years I met with each city manager and other officials from the city council trying to persuade the city to fulfill its obligations and responsibilities. Even the yard was in poor condition. It was obvious that the provisions of the transfer of the building to the city were not being honored. The condition of the building continued to decline. Something had to be done. No one was willing to recognize that if something were not done soon, the building would be lost forever.

The vestry of Christ Church was not interested in having another building to maintain. Christ Church had gone through a massive building program shortly after I arrived, and we were in the process of paying off the debt. And over the years, more property was purchased, and more building and expansion took place. So nothing happened with the old church, and with each passing year, the situation worsened.

In 1994, I asked Wylie Hogeman to see what he could do to help save the old church building. Wylie had been on the vestry when I came to Pensacola in 1966, had moved to Dayton, Ohio, and then retired and returned to Pensacola to take up where he had left off in the parish so many years before. I took Wylie to lunch at a restaurant at Seville Square and told him the problems of the old church with the city. He was interested and began to work behind the scenes with officials from the Historical Society, the Historic Pensacola Preservation Board, and the city manager. Then, suddenly, to everyone's surprise, in late 1995 the city and the Historic Pensacola Preservation Board began to discuss the possibility of a land swap, which would put the old church in the hands of the Historic Pensacola Preservation Board. The vestry of Christ Church, now concerned with the future of the old church, took a "wait and see" attitude with most feeling that the land swap would be a very good move. That proposal fell through, but by now the vestry was beginning to feel responsible for saving the building. The Historical Society had decided it wanted to buy the building, but the vestry and I felt it inappropriate for it to be up for sale. After all, Old Christ Church was our former home. It was, I insisted, our responsibility to save it and to restore it. In late 1995, the vestry was beginning to agree.

The city manager wrote a letter indicating the city did not have the money to restore and maintain the building even though it realized its responsibility to do so. In a February 1996 City Council Memorandum titled

PART FOUR, Old Christ Church 1867-1997

"Old Christ Church, Return to the Vestry of Christ Church," the city manager recommended: "That city council declare the city property known as Old Christ Church surplus and transfer the property by deed to the church wardens and vestrymen of Christ Church in Pensacola." The memo was signed by Edmond R. Hinkle, city manager.

Prior to this recommendation, the vestry of Christ Church had employed the engineering firm of Baskerville-Donovan to conduct a thorough study of what it would cost to bring the building up to code as well as what it would cost to completely restore it. The report was a shock to all concerned, especially the city council. The building was in much worse condition than we had thought. Baskerville-Donovan estimated it would cost an immediate $172,000 just to save the building and an additional $400,000 to completely restore it. The vestry passed this information on to the city manager, notifying the city that if these repairs were not forthcoming, then the vestry would exercise the reverter clause.

In the meantime, the *Pensacola News Journal* gave complete coverage to this, and several editorials were written in support of Christ Church regaining the title to the old church. And so, on Thursday evening, February 22, 1996, I asked the city council to return the building to Christ Church. I told the council that this was our former home, that three of our former rectors were buried under the building, that Old Christ Church was the oldest church building in Florida, and that the old church was in a dangerous state of repair and must be saved. I reminded them that the city did not want the building and that I was prepared to raise the funds to restore the building for the entire community as the center of the Historic Village and a place for concerts, recitals, lectures, and weddings. After some debate, the city council voted unanimously to return the building to "its rightful owner." When the vote took place, the mayor pro-tem, who was presiding, said, "On this historic occasion, instead of voting yes, let's vote Amen." And they did. And with that, after sixty years, Old Christ Church was back in the hands of Christ Church.

At that point, Wylie Hogeman, Roderic Magie, Robert P. Gaines, and I organized the Old Christ Church Foundation Inc., a corporation separate from the church wardens and vestry. We then asked the vestry to approve the foundation and to transfer the title of the old church to the foundation. The vestry approved and named nine trustees to run the new corporation. Then, after weeks of study and consultations with others in the community, the foundation leased the building to the state of Florida by way of the Historic Pensacola Preservation Board. In the fall of 1996, John Daniels, director of the preservation board, obtained a $307,000 grant from the state of Florida to help with the cost of restoration. The state legislature approved the grant in the spring of 1997. In response to the state grant, a three-year community fund drive was launched to raise the money to completely restore the the old church as it was in 1879 when the building was expanded twenty feet in the westerly direction.

✝

PART FIVE

The Search for the Lost Rectors, 1988

PART FIVE
The Search for the Lost Rectors, 1988

THE SEARCH FOR THE LOST RECTORS

"THE SEARCH FOR THE LOST RECTORS" WAS THE NAME the media gave to the project even before the official "groundbreaking" on Saturday, May 14, 1988. And it stuck. It was quite appropriate because that was the primary purpose of the archaeological investigation headed by Judith Bense, Ph.D., associate professor of anthropology at the University of West Florida and a nationally respected archaeologist. Cindy West, a reporter for the *Pensacola News Journal*, broke the story on Friday, May 6, 1988. The headline read, "Archaeologists Search for Lost Rectors." Her article began this way, "Archaeologists will spend the next two months digging up the past at Old Christ Church in Seville Square. Using their hands, shovels and trowels, excavators will try to find the bodies of three priests buried underneath the church where they're supposed to be—or in the church's backyard where they're not supposed to be. The dig will be led by Dr. Judy Bense, archaeologist at the University of West Florida. Archaeology students, members of the Pensacola Archaeological Society, and volunteers also will participate in what has become informally known as the 'Search for the Lost Rectors.'"

Two days before the groundbreaking ceremony, Earle Bowden, editor of

74 THE SEARCH FOR THE LOST RECTORS

Old Christ Church after 1879. (Courtesy of Christ Church Archives)

the *Pensacola News Journal*, wrote in a lead editorial titled "Digs Unfold Tapestry of History" the following: "The Search for the Lost Rectors sounds more like the title of a mystery novel than an archaeological dig in a church yard. But whatever it is called, the excavation under and around Old Christ Church should uncover some interesting artifacts of Pensacola history, as well as settle the question of whether the priests lie under the church as records indicate or were moved as local lore would have it."

The groundbreaking ceremony took place on a warm and beautiful Saturday, May 14, 1988. Many of those who would participate in the project were present along with representatives from the University of West Florida, Christ Church, the city and county, as well as a large number of interested citizens. John Daniels, director of the Historic Pensacola Preservation Board, presided on the porch of the Lear House, and I gave a short speech high-

PART FIVE, Search for the Lost Rectors, 1988

lighting the background of the project including a brief history of the early years of Christ Church. Other speakers were Dr. Bense, State Representative Tom Banjanin, and University of West Florida president, Dr. Morris Marx.

The text of my comments at the groundbreaking is included at this point because it helps tell the story of how things happened, what we were looking for, and the purpose of the historic archaeological investigation.

THE GROUNDBREAKING CEREMONY:
May 14, 1988

"Today is an historic day in the history of Pensacola, and I am glad to be a part of it. This event marks the official beginning of The Search for the Lost Rectors. It has a good ring to it, doesn't it? It is like a good mystery ... lost rectors, Civil War, Spanish treasures, Native American relics. There is no telling what lies underneath the surface of the ground just around the corner from the Lear House.

"And it all began in 1839 with the death of the Rev. Joseph Hubbard Saunders, rector of Christ Church. He was thirty-nine years old. He was buried under the vestry room of the church as an honor to him for his faithfulness in the pastoral care of his parishioners and others in this community who were dying of yellow fever. Seven years later, his successor, the Rev. Frederick Peake, died of consumption and was buried beneath the floor of the church. He was thirty-seven years old. Then in 1853, the Rev. David Flower died of yellow fever at the age of thirty-one and was buried under the chancel of the church.

"I have been under the church building ... not far mind you. There is nothing to indicate that they are there ... no markers, no marble slabs, nothing. In 1879, the west wall of the church was removed and the building was extended twenty feet. Under the church you can see the foundations of the old vestry room. These foundations are now under the present chancel.

"When I became the sixteenth rector of Christ Church in 1966, I visited the

museum in Old Christ Church as the guest of Miss Lelia Abercrombie and began a long and cherished friendship with her. She was also a parishioner of mine. Over the years she shared with me a story that I found intriguing. The story is that George Hallmark as a young boy witnessed the Union troops dig up the three rectors during the occupation of the city, perhaps looking for valuables which might have been interred with them. There is no record of this, but there are some records of what happened here during the Civil War. We know that the church building was used as a jail, barracks, and hospital during the occupation of the city. It would not be unusual for the graves to have been disturbed during the war. It happened all over the South and the North too, probably.

"George Hallmark later became a vestryman of Christ Church and was influential both in the parish and in the community of Pensacola for many years. Miss Abercrombie told me she had heard the story from her friend Daisy Hallmark, daughter of Judge Hallmark. And remember, too, that Miss Abercrombie in 1966 when she told me the story was only one generation removed from George Hallmark. Was the story true? Miss Abercrombie was certain of it. But no one could tell me that it was true other than Miss Abercrombie, but no one could prove it was not true either. And so I would ask those connected with the old church, 'Are the rectors buried under the church?' They would say 'Yes.' 'Are you certain of it?' And the answer, 'No.'

"I wanted to know for sure. And then, just a few weeks ago, I was informed by an attorney in my parish that when Old Christ Church was deeded to the city for a public library in 1936 by the vestry of Christ Church, forty feet west of the church property was not included in the transfer. Why? Was it a simple mistake, or was there a reason? Miss Abercrombie had been the prime mover behind getting the church building transferred to the city. Did she know something? Could it be that the rectors were buried on the forty feet retained by the vestry . . . or or even more interesting . . . is something else there?

"Two months ago, I shared these questions with a parishioner who said, 'Do you want to know?' I said, 'Yes,' and he replied, 'Call Judy Bense and if she will do a full and complete archaeological investigation, I will fund it.' It took no time to get her attention. She was even more excited about it than I. This is

PART FIVE, Search for the Lost Rectors, 1988

more than just 'The Search for the Lost Rectors.' This is a project on one of the most historic areas in Pensacola . . . not just Civil War and the early nineteenth century . . . but going back, like peeling an onion, to the Spanish period, the British period, and then the second Spanish period. And beyond that back to the time when the Indians walked these shores. What treasures there are just waiting to be found beneath the surface of the ground.

"To get the project going there were more things necessary than just a venture between the University of West Florida and Christ Church. Judy and I wanted this to be a community project, town and gown, believing that the best way to plan and build for the future is to understand and appreciate the past. Everybody with whom I have talked is excited, interested, and cooperative . . . John Daniels and the Historic Pensacola Preservation Board, who have gone above and beyond the call of duty; Jim Moody, the former director of the Historic Pensacola Preservation Board, who not only is a good friend and parishioner, but one who has kept my interest in the history of Pensacola alive for many years; Norman Simons, for many years curator of the museum in Old Christ Church, who keeps feeding me more information on the history of the city and Old Christ Church; Earle Bowden, editor of the Pensacola News Journal, who has enthusiastically supported and publicized this project and who has also given me generously of his time; Dr. Morris Marx, the president of the University of West Florida; the Pensacola Archaeological Society and the Treasure Hunters; and Cindy West of the Pensacola News Journal. All of these people, and all of these organizations, have evidenced the kind of enthusiasm that will guarantee the success of this project.

"If we find the lost rectors under the church where they were buried, we will suitably mark their graves. If they are on the forty feet outside the church we will, with dignity and care, place them where they were originally buried. This is an occasion for a deeper and richer look at our past, believing that the more we learn about our past history the better we will be in planning for our future. It is only when we know our past and understand and appreciate those who have come before us that we can build a better community. That is really what this is all about: to build a better community for our children and our children's children." —BMC

THE ARCHAEOLOGICAL INVESTIGATION BEGINS: MAY 16, 1988

When the archaeological investigation officially began on Monday, May 16, we did not know what we would find under the church building. It was a clear day and warm. It was perfect for the beginning of what would turn out to be an historic find. The professional archaeologists, the students, the volunteers, and the spectators were all filled with excitement. Dr. Bense thought the most likely place for the graves of the three rectors would be within the foundations of the old vestry room, and this would prove to be correct. But at the beginning no one was certain of anything except that this was quite a day for all of us.

It was difficult enough to excavate under the surface of the ground of the old vestry room. It would have been even more difficult if the graves had not been where Dr. Bense thought they were and we had to go further under the building. There was very little space between the floor of the church building and the ground level, and we had to enter through a very small opening at the west end of the building.

That first day was filled with excitement. Outside the building on the forty feet behind the church the students were hard at work digging artifacts from beneath the surface of the ground, artifacts from the British and Spanish colonial periods, including a good-luck medal. That was a very good omen. And from that day until the project was successfully completed we were blessed with good fortune.

BURIAL CHAMBER I DISCOVERED: MAY 17, 1988

On the second day of the investigation, Tuesday, May 17, shortly after four o'clock in the afternoon, a voice came from under the church,

PART FIVE, Search for the Lost Rectors, 1988

"We have found a human skull." I was there, and excitement swept the churchyard. Could it really be that one of the lost rectors' graves had been found this quickly into the project? A little later that same afternoon, it was confirmed. It was true, and remarkably the skull was only two inches under the ground. No one had expected to find anything that soon and certainly not that close to the surface. An arm bone was also uncovered. The humerus (the bone of the upper arm, from shoulder to elbow) was rotated 180 degrees. Al Taylor, a deputy sheriff and forensic specialist doing volunteer work for us, took a Polaroid picture for those of us in the backyard of the church. At that point I could no longer resist the urge to go under the building. Flat on my stomach, I literally rolled through the opening and into the area of the old vestry room. The opening was so small that you had to enter on your stomach on rollers that had been installed from the outside into the inner sanctum of the old church.

I must describe my feelings. Under the church and at this first burial chamber were Deborah Joy, the project director, and Mary Ann Fabbro, one of the staff archaeologists. Here in sight were the skeletal remains of one of my predecessors. At the time we mistakenly thought this was the Rev. Joseph Saunders. We would later learn that this was the Rev. David Flower, the youngest of the three lost rectors.

It was clear that this grave had been disturbed and the skull thrown back into the original grave. There was no top on the coffin. You could see the skull and the position of the humerus rotated 180 degrees. There were fragments of wood and nails. The first of the three lost rectors had been found. We were at the right place. But where were the other two?

I shall never forget the feeling of wonder and awe. The two archaeologists felt the same. I remembered what Jacob said so many thousands of years before when he wrestled with the angel: "How awesome is this place; this is none other than the house of God, and this is the gate of heaven" (Genesis 28: 16-17). There was a quiet and peace under that old church like I have seldom experienced. No one spoke. We just looked in amazement. Time stood still. David Flower had died of yellow fever, sacrificing his life for the flock he loved so dearly. And here, so many generations later was I, the sixteenth rector of his parish, actually seeing his skeletal remains. It was in the peace and quiet of that burial chamber that I resolved to find out all I could about him and the others. I also resolved that we would put things back in order when we had finished the investigation and conduct another funeral service, paying tribute once again to the three lost rectors and their sacrificial priesthood.

Dr. Bense was not present for this momentous discovery. She was teaching a class at the university but returned shortly. When she arrived she was thrilled, and her students were excited. She told me she was so glad I had been there when the grave was discovered, and then she asked, "What are you going to do with the remains when we finish?" I told her I wanted to have coffins made as much like the originals as possible and then have another burial using the 1789 *Book of Common Prayer*, which was used through most of the nineteenth century.

Gary Powell was also there when the grave was discovered. I had just met him but would come to know him well over the next weeks. Gary, a quadriplegic confined to a wheel chair, was a summer school student assigned to the project. He was unable to do the work of the students, but he had a keen mind and photographic memory. And because of these talents, Dr. Bense had assigned him the task of keeping a daily report, issuing a weekly news bulletin for visitors, and providing a running commentary for those who came to see what was taking place. He kept his records and became a fantastic tour guide. He told me, "I'm so glad you of all people were here when they found him." Gary would prove a valuable asset to the project with his remarkable memory for details and his interest in history. And his sense of humor carried us through some trying moments. He was an inspiration to all of us who were involved in the project. After it was over, what Gary saw at the funeral was one of the most remarkable events in my life.

By Wednesday, May 18, there was sufficient archaeological evidence to prove that the burial chamber had been disturbed prior to the addition of the west wall and the demolition of the vestry room in 1879. We were getting closer and closer to confirming the George Hallmark legend. Even if a

PART FIVE, Search for the Lost Rectors, 1988

young boy named George Hallmark had not seen the Union troops dig up the graves, somebody had done it. And it was done prior to 1879.

There was no reason to believe that the grave had been interfered with from the time of burial up to the evacuation of the city at the beginning of the Civil War. The vestry minutes did not mention anything of this nature. The *Pensacola Gazette* had no mention of grave robbers either before or after the war. Yet there are records from the Rev. John Jackson Scott after the war that the building had not only been badly damaged, but also that it had been desecrated. There are also records that one of the first things parishioners did upon return to the city was to repair the floor. In his report to the bishop of Florida in 1867, Dr. Scott wrote that his report was not complete because of a previous communication he had made to the bishop. This made us wonder if the desecration of the graves was so horrible that he and the bishop felt it best not to make it known to the general public out of respect to the families of the priests whose graves had been violated.

And so the archaeologists were prepared by Wednesday, May 18, to believe that this grave had been disturbed, that it had happened prior to 1879, that the top of the coffin had been pried off, and that the left humerus probably had been taken out of the coffin and then thrown back opposite from its normal position.

Now we were taking the George Hallmark legend seriously, and I was asked why I had believed it in the first place. As a theologian and student of Holy Scripture, it was easy for me to find truth in oral tradition, stories handed down from generation to generation. After all, parts of the Old Testament and the Gospels had begun in much this way. There had been no newspaper accounts of Jesus' life and teachings and no written record at the time of his ministry. The stories had been handed down in oral tradition for several years before Matthew, Mark, Luke, and John wrote them down. So, for me, there was no reason not to believe the George Hallmark story, especially when the person who told me was only one generation removed from Judge Hallmark, and his daughter was her friend. Why not believe it? Yes, Judy Bense had been right when she had said in a true scientific manner, "Let's look and see." That was precisely what was taking place. We were looking, and we were seeing much more quickly than we had anticipated.

On Thursday, May 19, the *Pensacola News Journal* ran a front-page story on the discovery of two days before. This three-column article written by Cindy West and the picture of the burial chamber created a flurry of excitement and interest through Pensacola. It would not be long before the "Search for the Lost Rectors" became news across the nation. In her article, West quoted Dr. Bense: "We have not seen remnants of the top of the coffin, but we have seen its side. The arm bone was upside down—the ball and socket joint at the shoulder was at the elbow and the elbow was at the jaw. This could be evidence that the rumor that Union troops destroyed and vandalized the priests graves was true." In this same article, Dr. Bense concluded, "This demonstrates archaeology is more than digging for goodies . . . it's an investigative procedure which can produce information in a unique way, just as many other investigative procedures can."

BURIAL CHAMBER II DISCOVERED: MAY 31, 1988

It was not until Tuesday, May 31 that the archaeologists found signs that another grave was located on the far side of the vestry room foundations. This would prove to be Burial Chamber II. This second grave was only three feet below the surface. What looked like the outline of a wooden vault began to appear. And then we experienced a severe problem. The archaeologists were dangerously near to the weight-bearing wall of the chancel of the church which had been added to the west wall with the expansion of the building in 1879. The problem was that if the vault lay beneath the weight-bearing wall, we were going to have a very difficult time getting to it. And for a fleeting moment I had the horrible thought that the newspaper might have the following headline the next day: "Old Christ Church Buries Archaeologists and Currin Beside Lost Rectors." But the next day

PART FIVE, Search for the Lost Rectors, 1988

UWF archaelology student Eric Duff uses a brush to clean the gravesite of the Rev. David Flower, the first of the three lost rectors found buried beneath Old Christ Church. (Photo by Gary McCracken, courtesy of *Pensacola News Journal*)

at least one third of the vault outline was exposed, and instead of it being under the weight-bearing wall, it was directly parallel to it. We were safe.

During the time the archaeologists were looking for Burial Chamber II, some of them were continuing to excavate the first burial chamber along with students and volunteers. Day by day more of the skeletal remains in Chamber I were being exposed. Outside the west wall, the earth from inside the building was being carefully sifted with artifacts being placed in plastic containers. Each container was labeled so the artifacts could be identified by chamber.

More wood fragments were coming out of Chamber II, as well as pottery and fragments of glass. It was becoming evident that the second burial chamber also had been vandalized. The deeper the excavation, the more rubble. On June 2, larger pieces of wood and a great deal of pottery were uncovered along with bone fragments, including a human vertebrae. By now they discovered the top of either a vault or coffin which had apparently sunken from the middle. The pieces of pottery, identified as belonging to the Spanish and British periods, were there when the church building was constructed in 1830-1832.

At the same time the Burial Chamber II was being excavated, the body in the first burial chamber was completely exposed. Preparations were made to remove the skeletal remains and take them to the lab at the university for further study. Pictures were taken, measurements were made, and each bone was removed, bagged in separate plastic containers, and carefully labeled. The bones would be reassembled at the university.

Concurrent with the work in both burial chambers and the sifting and labeling outside the west wall, plans were made to secure the weight-bearing wall as it was now assumed that the third burial chamber could well be directly under the wall and between the other two chambers. This would later prove to be incorrect. Not knowing for sure at that point, a structural engineer recommended by the city was asked for advice on how to excavate under the brick foundations without damaging the structure. The engineer suggested that a steel beam be placed on each side of the wall and then bolted together through the wall. It was assumed at that time and later

PART FIVE, Search for the Lost Rectors, 1988

substantiated that this 1879 brick support did not have any buried brick foundations to support it. The wall had been laid on top of the surface of the ground very likely to avoid disturbing the graves thought to be within the old vestry room foundations.

BURIAL CHAMBER III DISCOVERED: JUNE 13, 1988

By Wednesday, June 8, the skeletal remains in Chamber I had been removed, and the archaeologists were excavating deeper under the ground where the body had been. In Chamber II, part of a skull and some of the skeletal remains of the upper body could be seen. The skull was upside down. Some of the neck vertebrae were scattered. It was thought that some of the bone fragments found during the past few days may have been part of this skeleton. Then by late that afternoon the archaeologists found what appeared to be the edge of a third burial chamber partly under the support wall. This area did not seem to be disturbed, and the depth of this third chamber seemed to be the same depth as the second chamber, about four feet under the ground.

On Wednesday, June 22, the skeletal remains found in the third burial chamber were completely uncovered. There had been no disturbance in this grave and no indication of vandalism. The legend of George Hallmark was becoming more a reality. Maybe he had seen two of the three graves dug up and vandalized.

The skeletal remains in this chamber were in excellent condition. The outline of the coffin could be seen even though the wood had rotted long ago. From this chamber we were able to get the exact dimensions of the casket.

Never having been involved in an archaeological investigation, I was amazed at what could be revealed from the earth. It could be seen where the grave robbers had stopped digging only inches from the top of the coffin in this third chamber. Why did they stop? Why did they not dig down as deeply as they had in the second chamber? Did someone stop them or did they give up?

On Wednesday, June 22, Dr. Bense gave me another lesson in how archaeologists do their work. We went under the church building and looked at all three burial chambers. By now it was determined that the skeletal remains in the third burial chamber were in good enough condition to be removed and taken to the lab at the university, but the skeletal remains in the second chamber were so fragile that only the larger bones and skull could be removed for study. Once again, looking at the third burial chamber, I experienced the same feelings of wonder and awe that I had experienced at the two other chambers. But with this chamber, I had a much deeper feeling of peace and quiet. This chamber had not been disturbed.

During the entire time of the archaeological investigation, this same feeling of wonder and awe permeated those working under the building. There was never a moment when the archaeological team did not have the utmost respect for the remains of these three priests. They took their job seriously. They worked under extremely difficult conditions. It was impossible to stand up anywhere under the building. It was dry and hot even though air was piped under the church from the outside. Some days the temperature was in the high nineties outside the building.

A great deal of the enthusiasm and professionalism came from Dr. Bense. She instilled excellence in her staff, the students, and the volunteers. "The Search for the Lost Rectors" was coming to an end. They had been found. Many mysteries had been solved and questions answered, but the project was not at an end even though the major work under the building was winding down.

IDENTIFICATION OF THE SKELETAL REMAINS: JULY 8, 1988

Dr. Robert Daily, a forensic anthropologist from Florida State University in Tallahassee, spent Friday, July 8, with the staff and students at the University of West Florida. I was present, and it was a fascinating experience. Dr. Daily concluded that the identification of the skeletal remains in the burial chambers were as follows: Chamber I held the youngest of the three at the time of death (The Rev. David Flower). Chamber III was the oldest at the time of death (The Rev. Joseph Saunders), and Chamber II was between the youngest and the oldest in age (the Rev. Frederick Peake). He also noted that Joseph Saunders and Frederick Peake were each about five feet, ten inches tall and that David Flower was about five feet, eight inches tall. Some of the information we had from a diary of Joseph Saunders' father helped with the identification. You will find more about this in the section dealing with the biography of Joseph Saunders.

THE FUNERAL PREPARATIONS

We were now ready to make preparations for the funeral service to be conducted in the churchyard by the west wall of the church. Soon after the discovery of the first of the three priests, I talked with John Phillips III, a young master carpenter in the parish, and asked him if he would consider building the coffins. He was interested, and he made the coffins of red cedar, copies of the original ones. The original coffins were two inches wider at the widest point, but the new coffins had to be smaller in order to get through the small access to the burial chambers under the church building. That entrance was less than two feet wide and only eighteen inches high.

John spent three weeks constructing the toe-pincher coffins in the garage at his house. Needless to say this created some interest in the suburban area in which he lived, especially since there had been a murder a few blocks away only days before he started construction. Ben Morris of Harper-Morris Funeral Chapel and Don Nelson of Pensacola Marble and Granite provided the three marble grave stones inscribed with the names, date of death, age when they died, and identification that they had been rectors of

88 THE SEARCH FOR THE LOST RECTORS

Dr. Currin reads from the 1789 Book of Common Prayer during the funeral service for the lost rectors, July 23, 1988. Also pictured: Dr. Morris Marx (center) and John Phillips (right). Behind Phillips is the opening used by archaeologists to enter the burial chamber. (Photo by Gary McCracken, courtesy of *Pensacola News Journal*)

Christ Church. The marble markers also noted the date of the second burial, July 23, 1988. Dr. Bense had ceramic tablets made for each coffin, identifying each of the three lost rectors and briefly telling the story of the archaeological project.

Late in the afternoon before the funeral service, the coffins having been delivered to the Lear House behind the church, the skeletal remains were brought from the university to be placed in the coffins. Just as each bone had been placed in a separate plastic container and labeled and taken to the university, the same procedure was followed once again. The skeletons in their coffins spent the night there, and then early Saturday morning they were placed in the church building to lie in state until time for the service to begin.

PART FIVE, Search for the Lost Rectors, 1988

THE FUNERAL SERVICE: JULY 23, 1988

The weather on Friday had been terrible with high winds, lightning and heavy rain, and even though the weather prediction for Saturday was more of the same, it turned out to be a beautiful clear day and a bit cooler than it had been. The funeral began at ten o'clock with John Phillips, who had built the coffins, serving as the crucifer leading the procession from the nave of the old church through the great doors, down the steps to the sidewalk leading around the north side of the church to the backyard where the service would take place. The Christ Church choir and Ken Karadin, the church musician, processed immediately behind the crucifer who was carrying the large processional cross from Christ Church. Behind the choir, Dr. Morris Marx, president of the University of West Florida walked beside me, immediately ahead of the pallbearers. The pallbearers were archaeologists and students who had worked on the project the past two months. Gary Powell was following us in his wheelchair beside the procession. A few weeks later he would startle me when he asked me about the three "church clergymen" who were walking behind Dr. Marx and me and in front of the caskets. He obviously saw three men in white no one else saw.

We had several hundred people turn out for the service, far more than I had expected. There were many members of Christ Church as well as many who had been connected with the project. But there were also a large number of Pensacola citizens and others who had come from out of town. The project had indeed caught the attention of many across the nation. Articles had appeared in newspapers across the country, and television had reported on the project. Even Cable News Network covered part of the dig.

The service was from the Burial Office from the 1789 *Book of Common Prayer*, which would have been the service used for the burial of the three rectors at the time of their death. The 1789 *Book of Common Prayer* was not revised until 1892. Hymns of that day and age were sung. After the

John Phillips assists in placing one of the caskets into the burial chamber beneath Old Christ Church. This was the entrance used by the archaeologists to get under the church. (Photo by Gary McCracken, courtesy of *Pensacola News Journal*)

service was concluded and the congregation had departed, I went under the church for the final time and consecrated the graves which had been prepared the previous week. The coffins were then placed under the church in their final resting place. The following week, the graves were filled with earth, cement was poured on the top of the ground over them, and the marble stones were embedded in the fresh cement. The project had been successful beyond our highest expectations.

†

PART SIX

The Lost Rectors

Joseph Hubbard Saunders, 1800-1839

Frederick Foote Peake, 1809-1846

David Dubois Flower, 1822-1853

PART SIX
The Lost Rectors

JOSEPH HUBBARD SAUNDERS: 1800-1839

WHEN THE REV. JOSEPH HUBBARD SAUNDERS BECAME the first rector of Christ Church in 1836, he faced many challenges. From 1829, with the incorporation of the parish by the Territorial Legislature, missionary priests from the General Missionary Society of the Episcopal Church had preceded him: Addison Searle, Benjamin Hutchins, and Ashbel Steele, under whose leadership the church building had been completed in 1832. For nearly three years the parish had been without a full-time priest, and Pensacola was a small city with only Key West as its rival in size, both having little more than 2,000 inhabitants. Christ Church had only twenty-one communicants. There were, by the time of his arrival in the city, several clergymen attempting to establish churches. However in 1838, Mr. Saunders reported that he was the only Protestant clergyman in the city.

Mr. Saunders came to Pensacola with the best of credentials. He was born on December 26, 1800, to a prominent North Carolina family. James Saunders and Hannah Citterzen Simons were his parents. His mother was a widow when she married her second husband. Young Joseph grew up in the country outside Edenton, North Carolina, and until he was fourteen, he was educated there. He was then placed in "the Academy" in Raleigh, North Carolina, where he remained for forty months before entering the sophomore class at the University of North Carolina at Chapel Hill in 1819. His mother died when he was nineteen. Joseph graduated from the University of North Carolina with a B.A. degree on June 7, 1821. He stayed at the university as a tutor in English and history while he studied law, and he received an M.A. degree in 1824.

Joseph's father wrote about the family and Joseph in particular. In "A Genealogical Table for the use of Joseph H. Saunders; written by his Father, James Saunders, Town of Edenton, North Carolina, A.D., 1824," Joseph's father describes his son: "He is about six feet high, weighing about two hundred pounds, rather of a dark complexion, dark hair, and eyes between dark and light. He does not stand so straight and elegant as I could wish him, but this I think may be owing to his having been delving over books so long, and that when he comes to turn out in the world and feels the necessity of demeaning himself agreeable to the custom and prevailing fashion of the times, he will improve his present posture of standing and sitting, for when he was growing up I thought him as handsome and well formed a youth as any whatever; and O, may he become and remain everything I wish him. He certainly has hitherto by his life, dutiful behavior and perseverance in his studies; merited my warmest approbation."

His father died on June 22, 1824, and young Joseph resigned his tutorship at the university and studied law under Judge Francis Nash. But he soon abandoned that in order to study theology. During these years he taught school in Edenton. In 1866, Joseph Saunders' son added as an "Addenda to the Manuscript of James Saunders" that the reason Joseph taught school was due to "the insolvent condition (I presume) of his father's estate requiring his presence and necessitating immediate exertion on his part. He appropriated the proceeds of his own labor to the payment of his father's debts."

The year 1831 was the beginning of a new life for Joseph Saunders. He was ordained deacon by the Rt. Rev. Richard C. Moore, bishop of Virginia, on February 6, 1831, and on March 18, 1832, he was ordained

PART SIX, The Lost Rectors

to the priesthood by the Rt. Rev. Levi S. Ives, bishop of North Carolina, in Warrenton, North Carolina. The following year, April 25, he married Laura Lucinda, daughter of Dr. Simmons J. Baker of Martin County, North Carolina. They had four children. Richard Benbury was born in Raleigh, North Carolina, April 12, 1834. William Laurence was also born in Raleigh on July 30, 1835. Ann was born in Pensacola, April 26, 1837, and Joseph Hubbard Jr. was born on October 23, 1839, the day before his father died.

And so when the Rev. Joseph Saunders moved to Pensacola in the fall of 1836, he had two small children. Having lived in Raleigh and at the University of North Carolina at Chapel Hill, he must have felt he had really come to the mission field in a frontier town. His call to Christ Church must have excited him. The vestry not only wanted a rector, they also wanted him to establish a school, and he had previously had a lot of experience in that field. From the *Pensacola Gazette* dated March 3, 1838, we read an advertisement for the Pensacola Academy: "The high character of their principal, who, for fifteen years has been engaged in the education of youth, the unrivaled salubrity of the climate of Pensacola, and its growing importance and increasing facilities of communication with the adjacent states, embolden the trustees of the Pensacola Academy, to recommend it to parents, guardians, and others, and to solicit for it that patronage which it merits."

An accompanying article contains a recommendation of Joseph Saunders from Walker Anderson, former professor at the University of North Carolina, and now on the vestry of Christ Church. Mr. Anderson states that Mr. Saunders acquired a reputation at the University of North Carolina "of being one of the best officers ever attached to the university." Walker Anderson and Joseph Saunders had known one another at the university, and Mr. Anderson over the years became one of the staunchest members of Christ Church, serving on the vestry for many years as senior warden and as a lay reader. He eventually became chief justice of the Florida Supreme Court. He continued his close friendship with the Saunders family after Joseph's death. One of Richard Benbury Saunders' children was named Walker Anderson after their family friend.

Two years after his arrival in Pensacola, the Diocese of Florida was organized due in large measure to Mr. Saunders' leadership. The Primary Convention was called to meet at St. John's Church in Tallahassee for the stated purpose of organizing the Diocese of Florida as part of the Protestant Episcopal Church in the United States of America. Judge John Cameron of Christ Church wrote the Constitution and Canons for the new diocese, and Joseph Saunders presided at the convention. There were only seven churches in Florida, and three priests were in attendance: Mr. Saunders from Christ Church; the Rev. Robert Dyce, rector of St. Paul's, Key West; and the Rev. J. Loring Woart, rector of St. John's, Tallahassee. There were twelve lay delegates from the churches with no representation from St. John's, Jacksonville. The other churches were St. John's, Jacksonville; Trinity, St. Augustine; Trinity, Apalachicola; and St. Joseph's, St. Joseph, Florida. The town of St. Joseph and the church were destroyed by the hurricane of 1841.

Another highlight of Mr. Saunders' rectorship of the parish, which took place the following month, was the Episcopal visitation to the parish by the Rt. Rev. Jackson Kemper, missionary bishop of Missouri and Indiana. He came to consecrate the church building and to administer the apostolic rite of confirmation. This was the first Episcopal visitation in Northwest Florida. Bishop Kemper arrived in the city on Shrove Tuesday, February 27, 1838, and remained for six days. He stayed with Judge John Cameron, the uncle of Mrs. Walker Anderson. In his diary, Bishop Kemper writes of Mr. and Mrs. Saunders as a "worthy couple."

In that same diary, Bishop Kemper describes his entrance into Pensacola Bay after setting sail from Mobile. "Saw umbrella pines which made a pretty appearance. Most of the wood in sight is pines. Gulls, pelicans and bald eagles flying about . . . a large company of pelicans standing on the shore near the mouth of Rio Perdido which separates Alabama from Florida. The Bay of Pensacola is considered one of the finest on the gulf. The sun was set when we entered it. It is purely inter-

PART SIX, The Lost Rectors

locked at the entrance on the capes of which are two large forts and near the one on the right hand a merchant vessel lately lost by a drunken pilot, a naval hospital, a revolving lighthouse, the Navy Yard arrested our attention, and at seven o'clock we landed at the end of a very long wharf. Judge Cameron insisted on taking me to his house. Mr. Saunders, the rector, was sent for, and I passed a pleasant evening."

Bishop Kemper's description of Pensacola in 1839 is quite interesting. He writes: "This town has quite a novel appearance. It contains about 2,200 inhabitants and is situated on one of the finest bays in the world. The houses have a foreign appearance similar I suppose to those in the South of Europe. It is actually built on a bed of sand, yet the inhabitants make out to have something like gardens. I have seen fig trees as large as apple trees."

The bishop's stay in Pensacola was somewhat disappointing. The weather was terrible, the bishop had an intestinal upset, and attendance at church services was small. The storm was so intense that the consecration of the church building on the first Sunday in Lent, March 4, 1838, had to be delayed until noon, and there were only five in attendance. At three-thirty that afternoon, Bishop Kemper confirmed ten people. There was a third service that evening at seven-thirty.

In his diary, Bishop Kemper, reflecting on the church in Pensacola, writes: "Almost everything it appears to me is to be done here." Of his cold, he writes: "I resorted to antimonial wine and was made exceedingly sick by it." He notes that eighteen received communion that first Sunday in Lent and that several of other denominations were present and "united with us." And then he adds, "What could have led to our establishment of a church here. For even yet apart from the judge's relatives there are scarcely any Episcopalians here. Scarcely any officers ever in the church. Still Saunders has a good field before him. And if this new city is to be built up, he will in time have a fine congregation."

Is it possible that Judge Cameron was ready for the bishop to leave? Bishop Kemper writes this about his departure: "I have a difficulty about my journey. Almost everyone appears to think the road is impassable.

Not so the judge, who appears all but determined that I shall go tonight.... As soon therefore as the third service was over I packed my robes and hastened to the boat where Mr. Saunders joined me. We started at half past ten o'clock." As the bishop leaves Pensacola, he again describes what he sees. "We are on Santa Rosa Inlet. The island S.R. is said to be peculiar for its purely white sands and occasional green spots. The sand is so white that you can see from the boat the footsteps of the deer and birds." And almost as an afterthought he adds: "The Gospel must be taken to the sailors of our Navy."

In his annual report to the Diocese of Florida for that year, Mr. Saunders writes about the inclusiveness of the parish: "They have therefore taken different ways to cause the church to be regarded, not as any party concern whatever, but as the divinely constituted society for the salvation of all men's souls; to whose benefits and offices all, without exception, were equally entitled: and in pursuance of the idea they have endeavored to have it distinctly understood among all classes of the population that the rector would be glad, not only to instruct in church all who would attend, but also to visit all of every race in society at their houses; to baptize their infants, catechize their children, visit their sick, bury their dead, and render them pastoral services in any way within his power. In these efforts, the friends of the church have met with so much success as to feel that it is clearly their duty to continue them."

Mr. Saunders' ministry was not limited to the white population. He established mission work for the black population as well. In his report to the diocese he writes that "the rector, with the advice and recommendation of the vestry, established a weekly service and sermon on Sunday afternoon for the black people, when the white families, at the suggestion of the vestry, cheerfully gave up their pews to their servants, while those gentlemen who attend sit in the gallery."

In his last report to the diocese, Mr. Saunders again speaks of the ecumenical nature of Christ Church. He reports that "there are about ten Presbyterians, Congregational and Methodist communicants, who are uniform and exemplary partakers at the altar, have pews in church,

PART SIX, The Lost Rectors

and contribute cheerfully to its support."

That year, 1838, was indeed quite a year for Mr. Saunders. He had been a major participant in the formation of the new diocese. He had hosted the first Episcopal visitation to Pensacola, and the church building was now consecrated. Then in September, he came very close to being elected missionary bishop of Arkansas.

The Rev. Huston Horn of Pasadena, California, an authority on the life of Bishop Leonidas Polk, has a copy of a September 15, 1838 letter written by Joseph Saunders to his wife from the General Convention of the Episcopal Church in Philadelphia where he was a clerical deputy from the Diocese of Florida. It reads:

My dearest and beloved wife,

The convention has now got so far through its business that I think I can see the end, and we shall probably adjourn on Monday next, or on Tuesday morning, though the former will, I think, be the day. I shall directly after the adjournment go to New York and get through my business there as soon as possible, for I long to be home, and to press you, my dearest, to my bosom, and to hear your voice and to see your face, as well as to see the dear children.

Today I had a rich treat. I got four letters from the post office, two from you, one from Mr. Walker Anderson, and one from your father. I'd gone so many days to the post office without getting a letter from my dear wife that I had become uneasy lest some of you were sick, but this morning I was richly repaid for all your letters were, of course, interesting, not the least so the part relating to the Warrenton offer. Your pa's was on the same subject, for I wrote to him the day after I got here requesting his advice on the offer. I had breakfast at Mr. White's the morning I came through Warrenton and was informed that the letter had been written.

But I have had more weighty matters to decide. The Bishops determined last Saturday or Monday to nominate a missionary bishop for Arkansas, the only remaining part of the South-West which has not been formed into a Diocese. On Tuesday last, I believe, Bishop Ives informed me that he had proposed me to the House of Bishops as a suitable person for the appointment. This thing did not take me altogether by surprise. I told the objections which had occurred to me and requested that he would drop my name; still it was spoken of during the week, and this morning Bishop Ives called me out of the House of Deputies and informed me that the bishops had fixed upon twelve o'clock today on the hour for proceeding to the election and that he had come to see me at the request of some of the bishops. I reminded him of my former statement, urged him to express my thanks for the good opinion which had been formed of me, but assured him that I could not accept the appointment and recommended Leonidas Polk, who had also been spoken of. Under the aspect which the business has assumed, I did not feel it to be my duty to accept and to remove you and the children to Arkansas. In this determination I thought I would be obliging you, but the reasons and all the circumstances, which are pretty long, I will state when I see you.

Polk was finally nominated unanimously by the bishops, and on the nomination being communicated to the House of Deputies, I moved, after some remarks, in favor of it and stating to the house that I had been acquainted with him for more than twenty years (that goes back to 1818 when I was eighteen years old), that the house proceed to the election by ballot, whereupon he was unanimously chosen by the House of Deputies. I have my fear that he will not accept, but time will determine. Kiss the children and may the Lord bless you, my own true love. J.H. Saunders.

A little more than one year later, Joseph Saunders died of yellow fever on Thursday, October 24, 1839, at the age of thirty-nine and was buried that same afternoon. The floor of his vestry room was removed, and he was buried near the spot in which he was in the habit of sitting. This story appears in the *Pensacola Gazette*, the *Journal of the Diocese of Florida*, the Saunders family genealogy, and in a letter written by Walker Anderson. This letter is so significant that it is included here.

PART SIX, The Lost Rectors

Pensacola, Florida, October 27, 1839

My dear Sir:

It has been a long time since we interchanged a letter, and it is a sad occasion that prompts me to renew our correspondence. We have lost a beloved and valued friend, and I know it will afford you a mournful pleasure to learn some particulars of his last hours. Our excellent pastor, The Reverend Mr. Saunders, has been removed from his labors on earth to his reward in heaven and left a whole community in tears. He died on Thursday morning, the twenty-fourth instant, after a distressing illness of eight days with a malignant brain fever. You have heard doubtless of the terrible scourge with which our neighbor, Mobile, has been visited this fall. Among the fugitives from that place many came here, and bringing the seeds of disease with them, they came only to linger and die among strangers. There were, therefore, many calls upon the sympathy of all; none responded to such calls more freely than our dear friend. He was continually aboard day and night with the sick and dying, exposing himself fearlessly to the sun and the dews. On Sunday before his illness commenced he preached at the request of the commodore of the squadron here on board of the flagship, and on his return complained that he felt the sun beating powerfully on his head as he was preaching; for the service was on the deck, and his being elevated brought his head near to the awning, which was between them and the sun. Though he felt his head affected from this time he did not complain much of it, and on Tuesday night, being called up at midnight to visit a young lady who was dying with yellow fever, he went, having to walk near a half mile in a high, keen wind. He was up the whole night and spoke to me afterward of the severe trial of feeling he underwent from the painful circumstances of the death-bed he attended. On Wednesday morning at nine o'clock he was taken with a chill, followed by high fever. From the first he had the best medical advice, the fleet surgeons from both the American and French squadrons being assiduous in their attention, and I need not say he was nursed as faithfully as the most devoted love could dictate by his anxious and sorrowing people. His disease at first seemed to be a common bilious fever, such as has prevailed lately to some extent among us, but which is usually mild and easily managed, and in his case it seemed to yield readily to the prescriptions, but on Monday we began to perceive indications of an affection of the brain, and during that night we could no longer mistake the malignant character of the attack.

On Thursday morning after waking from a sleep of some hours his mind was greatly obscured, and before that night came, a dismal darkness had settled over his fine and well-balanced intellect. He raved incessantly and incoherently, but in all his wanderings God and Christ and heaven was the burden of his thoughts. He was ever going through some of the services of the church or in a loud and anxious tone extorting his people. He would call on us to pray and with a devout and impassioned manner repeat scraps from the Prayer Book, and once he got as far in the Lord's Prayer as the petition "Thy will be done." This continued with but little intermission for forty-eight hours, for even when his strength failed him by bending your ear to his lips, you find he still was whispering about the church and kindred topics. He sunk to rest without apparent suffering, though while his extremities were chilling with the damps of death, the heat of the top of his head was almost painful to touch. Not a single glimmering of reason was permitted to cheer those who watched his parting struggle. He was buried on the afternoon of Thursday with more than the ordinary marks of respect. The floor of his vestry room was removed, and his grave dug beneath the spot in which he was in the habit of sitting when there. The vestry, besides addressing a letter of condolence to his widow, full of admiration for his character and sorrow for his loss, have determined to erect a tablet to his memory. So universal was the reverence in which he was held that on the day of his death and funeral the stores of the whole city were closed, the Creoles and Catholics uniting heartily with his own people in this demonstration of respect, and the officers of the French Squadron, which is lying in our harbor, attended the services in full uniform.

The *Pensacola Gazette* published a tribute to him in its edition of November 2, 1839. Of his three years as rector of Christ Church, the newspaper stated, "Failing in nothing which the solemn responsibilities of his sacred office demanded, his faithful rebukes were yet blended with such gentleness of manner, such affectionate interest in the objects of care as his to win the hearts of all with whom he came in contact, while the unsullied purity of his life extorted admiration from all... To the poor, the sick, and the sorrowing, his attentions were unwearied. In this season of unusual peril he shrunk not from exposure to the midday sun nor to the midnight dews, and he thus fell a martyr to the cause he loved best, that of soothing the griefs of this world and leading to the felicities of the next. He went down to an honored grave amidst the lamentations of his bereaved congregation, leaving for their example a character full of those virtues which adorn this life and sanctify their possessor for a better. He died in the thirty-ninth year of his age, leaving a widow and four infant children. His remains were deposited under the vestry room of Christ Church, in this city."

Joseph Saunders' fourth child, Joseph Hubbard, was born the day before he died and was named after his father. Laura Lucinda, his widow, moved to Jackson County, Florida, where her father, Dr. Baker, had a home. They stayed there for six months before moving back to Raleigh, North Carolina. They remained in Raleigh until July 1850 when they moved to Chapel Hill so Richard and William could enter the freshman class at the University of North Carolina.

All three of Mr. Saunders' sons rose to prominence in North Carolina. We know nothing of his daughter. His sons graduated from the University of North Carolina with M.A. degrees like their father. William Laurence also received his law degree and an honorary LL.D. degree from the university. Richard Benbury became a highly respected and prosperous chemist (druggist) and businessman in Chapel Hill. William Laurence practiced law, was a newspaper publisher, and was for many years Secretary of State of North Carolina. Joseph Hubbard was a prosperous land-owner and planter. All three sons served with distinction in the Confederate Army during the Civil War. William Laurence served under Gen. Robert E. Lee and was wounded twice. He was present at Lee's surrender at Appomattox. Richard Benbury married the daughter of the governor of Mississippi and settled in Chapel Hill. William Laurence lived first in Salisbury and then in Tarboro, North Carolina, where he is buried. Joseph Hubbard was twice wounded in the Civil War, seriously at the Battle of Gettysburg. He was captured by the Union Army and remained a prisoner until March 1865 when he was paroled for exchange and returned to Chapel Hill. Laura Lucinda, widow of Joseph Saunders, died in Chapel Hill on October 23, 1881. She never re-married. One of the oldest buildings on the campus of the University of North Carolina bears the name Saunders Hall.

FREDERICK FOOTE PEAKE 1809-1846

Frederick Peake decided to leave Christ Church in St. Louis, Missouri, in 1842 because of his declining health. He had contracted a serious lung ailment and believed that perhaps the warm climate and fresh air from the Gulf might help. He had consumption or tuberculosis, and he had no way of knowing that his life would be very short indeed. Nevertheless, with faith and determination, he and his family moved to Pensacola. He knew the fate of his precedessor Joseph Saunders, but the prospects of yellow fever did not deter him. He was excited about his new parish and especially the desire of the vestry and others in the community to establish a school for the youth of this small city. Christ Church, St. Louis, is today the Cathedral Church for the Episcopal Diocese of Missouri and in Peake's day was already a church with great potential.

The *Pensacola Gazette* reported on November 26, 1842: "We are requested to say that the Reverend Mr. Peake, late Rector of Christ Church, St. Louis, will preach at the Episcopal Church tomorrow morning at the usual hour." This was obviously good news for Pensacola because there had been no resident rector since the Rev. Joseph Saunders died in

PART SIX, The Lost Rectors

1839. During the next three years, the parish had been served by visiting clergymen when they could be found.

Even though gravely ill, Frederick Peake went to work with great vigor and determination. The year following his arrival, the *Journal of the Diocese of Florida* reported that he was holding services twice each Sunday and every Holy Day. He further reported that funds were being given by members of the parish for the establishment of an educational institution for young people and that such a school had already begun under his direction. He also reported that within the year there were already seventy pupils in the school.

The Collegiate Institute, also called the Pensacola Collegiate Institute, had officially opened in January following Peake's arrival, and by 1844, it was flourishing and growing rapidly. He was the principal, and there were three teachers. The school issued a catalog which is thought to be the first of its kind of any school in Florida. In those days in Pensacola as well as throughout the nation, the education of the youth was an important part of the ministry and mission of the church.

Also, during this period of time, the Rev. Charles Peake, brother of Frederick, moved to Pensacola to assist his brother both in the parish and in the Collegiate Institute. He had been ordained to the priesthood shortly before his arrival in Pensacola by the bishop of Alabama, the Rt. Rev. Nicholas H. Cobbs, who from time to time visited Christ Church to administer the Apostolic Rite of Confirmation.

Doubtless Charles Peake came to Pensacola to try to take some of the strain off of his older brother, who was both rector and principal of the school. Frederick Peake had now but two years before his untimely death, and yet he continued to work and minister to the needs of a growing parish and school.

Frederick Foote Peake was a man of great intellect and dedication. Doubtless he knew his time was running out, and he wanted to accomplish as much as possible for the church and the people he loved and served with such distinction. He was graduated from the General Theological Seminary in New York City on July 2, 1836, the year Joseph

Saunders came to be rector of Christ Church. He was ordained deacon by the Rt. Rev. Benjamin T. Onderdonk, the bishop of New York, two days after graduation. Three years later, on April 1, 1839, he was ordained to the priesthood by the Rt. Rev. Jackson Kemper, missionary bishop of Missouri and Indiana.

His first parish was Christ Church, Booneville, Missouri, serving under Bishop Jackson Kemper where it was reported at the time of Peake's death that his "influence for good is still felt." It is interesting that this is the first of three Christ Churches he would serve. From Booneville he moved to Fayette serving St. Mary's Church, and then he returned to Booneville. From there, he went to Christ Church, St. Louis.

It was said that he was the kind of priest who was attractive to the young, and he was young himself when he came to Pensacola. He was handsome, articulate and the kind of person who manifested a deep spirituality. A letter written by J. W. Dunn to the Rev. M. Schuyler in Lexington, Kentucky, contains a glowing report of Peake's ministry even before his coming to Pensacola. "Particularly attractive to the young, the interest he manifested in their spiritual and temporal affairs soon won their hearts," the letter said. "Many got their first impressions of the church and imbibed their love for it and for him."

That same attractiveness and charm made him a well-known figure in Pensacola. But his time was running out, and in the prime of his life, the fatal lung disease took his life. He died on November 27, 1846, having been in Pensacola but four years. His death was one of great agony, but he faced it with the faith and courage of a true and dedicated priest of the Church.

The *Pensacola Gazette* recorded it this way on November 28, 1846: "Yesterday morning we were called on to mourn the departure from among us of the Rev. Frederick F. Peake. He had been long afflicted with a pulmonary complaint, and his spirit had at last taken flight for that blest abode, of whose holiness of life; on earth had been one continued illustration. It is not often that we indulge in the language of eulogy or panegyric; it is not often that such language is meet or proper;

PART SIX, The Lost Rectors

Frederick Foote Peake (1809-1846). (Photo of a portrait given to Christ Church, St. Louis, Missouri, by his family. Courtesy of Christ Church Archives)

it is, in general, sufficient that the tears of bereaved survivors moisten the grave of the departed; sufficient, that his virtues be held in kindly and unfading remembrance around the family altar. But there are occasions of more widespread grief, occasions on which the voice, not of sympathy alone, but of mourning and lamentation, goes up from every heart. Such is the present occasion. If there ever lived a man of high attainments and uncommon power of mind, void of all worldly desire for wealth, position, or renown—that man was the subject of this brief notice. He made his home among us upwards of four years ago and fondly hoped that he had here found a refuge against his fearful malady.

But death had marked him for his own. None knew this better than the deceased—none with more Christian philosophy than he, looked forward to the closing scene of his earthly existence; yet he labored on, in his holy calling and in the instruction of youth, as if he had an appointed task, that must be done while it was yet day, and before the night of the grave should close upon him. In his life and in his death, he exemplified the beautiful adage that

> "'Tis not the whole of life to live,
> Nor all of death, to die.
> "'Peace to his ashes! Honor to his memory!
> Reader, he was your brother.'

"The funeral of the late Rev. Frederick F. Peake will take place tomorrow morning (Sunday, November 29, 1846). The bell will toll one hour before the procession moves from his late residence."

Mr. J. W. Dunn in his letter to the Rev. M. Schuyler describes Mr. Peake's untimely death. "In his last hour he was perfectly composed and cheerful; he sat up in bed and conversed calmly with the physician who was attempting to stop the hemorrage which was flowing profusely from his lungs. His dear wife, who saw that he was fast fading away, asked him if he was not comforted; he replied, 'Yes, in Christ—all, all in Christ Jesus!' As I stood by the bedside of that dying saint, the one thought that came to my mind, and has since almost daily come for upward of twenty years was, 'Let me die the death of the righteous.'"

And so, the second of the three Lost Rectors died having served the parish and the Lord he loved with total devotion and commitment. The final note from the *Pensacola Gazette* on May 15, 1847, is a sad one indeed: "Will those persons, who have in their possession, books belonging to the library of the late Reverend F. Peake, confer a favor upon Mrs. Peake by leaving them at her residence." And from a port of Pensacola report dated June 12 that same year comes the end of the

PART SIX, The Lost Rectors   109

story: "The following passengers sailed Tuesday last—Mrs. Peake (wife of the late Rev. Frederick F. Peake) and child, and Master William Dorr."

Frederick Peake's family sailed away, never to return. The Rev. Mr. Peake had been buried beneath the floor of the church beside his predecessor, the Rev. Joseph Saunders. A second memorial tablet was made and installed in the wall of the church building by the vestry of Christ Church.

> FAITHFUL UNTO DEATH
> SACRED
> TO THE MEMORY OF
> REV. FREDERICK F. PEAKE
> LATE RECTOR OF THIS CHURCH
> WHO DEPARTED THIS LIFE
> NOV. 27th, 1846
> AGED 37 YEARS
> "HE RESTS FROM HIS LABORS, AND HIS WORKS
> DO FOLLOW HIM"

THIS STONE IS ERECTED BY HIS SORROWING CONGREGATION, AS A MEMORIAL OF THEIR AFFECTIONATE REGARD, "BLESSED ARE THE DEAD WHO DIE IN THE LORD, EVEN SO SAITH THE SPIRIT FOR THEY REST FROM THEIR LABORS"

From the parish register of the time of Frederick and Charles Peake we find the names of those who would continue to be leaders of Christ Church for many generations. Some of them were Hyer, Dorr, Baker, Caldwell, and Chase as well as Anderson, Campbell, Avery, Knowles, Cameron, Blount, Willis, Drake, and Brosnaham. We also find that the church and the priests in particular ministered to the black people in the community with baptisms and marriages and funerals.

DAVID DUBOIS FLOWER—1822-1853

When David Flower came to Pensacola to become rector of Christ Church the future never looked better for him. He was young, recently married, had a theological degree from the General Theological Seminary in New York City, and he and his wife were eagerly expecting their first child. David Flower died ten weeks later on September 10, 1853, at 8:30 p.m., a victim of yellow fever at the age of thirty-one. His wife, Lucy, died eleven days later, and his infant son, born five days after his father's death, died on September 30. Yellow fever claimed the lives of the entire Flower family during one of the worst of the yellow fever epidemics that took the lives of so many in Pensacola.

David Dubois Flower was born on November 15, 1822, in South Hempstead, New York. He was baptized on May 23, 1824. He was the third of eight children. Of his early years we know nothing, but we do know that he graduated in 1847 from the General Theological Seminary in New York, one of the finest theological seminaries on the East Coast, and he was ordained deacon in the Episcopal Church on June 27, 1847. From New York, he went to Jacksonville, Alabama, far from his home at the age of twenty-five, to become the first resident minister of what was then an unorganized congregation later to be named St. Luke's Church.

Ronald J. Caldwell, professor of history at Jacksonville State University in Jacksonville, Alabama, and a communicant of St. Luke's Church, gives us some interesting insights into the early ministry of Mr. Flower, the founding rector of that church. "By all accounts David Dubois Flower was the very personification of Christian virtue and devotion. Bishop Nicholas H. Cobbs said of him, 'He was an humble, faithful, devoted man, adorning the doctrine of his Lord and Master by a holy walk and conversation. His Christian character was consistent and lovely in an eminent degree.' Other witnesses testified to his meek,

PART SIX, The Lost Rectors 111

humble, and holy life and his selfless and complete devotion to Christian service. It is no wonder that he was highly regarded and deeply loved by the people whose lives he touched. Simply stated, he was a saintly man."

Mr. Flower was but twenty-five years old when he began his new ministry in Alabama in 1847. And what an undertaking it must have been for him, far from home, with a handful of people (four communicants of the Church), no church building, and no rectory. He was paid $5.34 per month. The next year, the young deacon attended the convention of the Diocese of Alabama, meeting in Mobile and reported, "I feel confident that the church can be established in this place by perseverance. 'In quietness and confidence is our strength.'" The young deacon must have been persuasive and hardworking for St. Luke's Church, Jacksonville, Alabama, was admitted into union with the Diocese of Alabama on May 4, 1849.

Two years after his ordination as deacon, David Flower was ordained to the priesthood in the Episcopal Church in Huntsville, Alabama, by the Rt. Rev. Nicholas Hooker Cobbs on July 9, 1848. In 1851, Mr. Flower resigned as rector. In the thirtieth year of his life, he married Lucy Coles Winston in Columbus, Lowndes County, Mississippi. His wife was born in Culpeper County, Virginia, in 1815 and was the daughter of a wealthy planter there. She had moved to Lowndes County, Mississippi, to live at the home of her brother.

After serving as rector of Saint Stephen's Church in Eutaw, Alabama, for a short time, he moved to Mobile and became the founder of St. John's Church there under the direction of the rector of Trinity Church. He remained in Mobile for only a few months, having become disheartened from the lack of encouragement for the establishment of a church there. From there, he accepted the call in 1853 to become rector of Christ Church, Pensacola, Florida, following the Rev. John Jackson Scott, who had served the parish for five years and had resigned to enter the military as a chaplain.

These must have been exciting times for the young priest and his wife, Lucy. Christ Church was a stable and well-known parish with tremendous potential for growth, and the stately church building was only twenty-one years old and in a prominent location. David and Lucy set up housekeeping, ordering from New Orleans a double bed with cornice, a breakfast table, an enclosed wash-stand, and a cane-back nursing chair.

The Flowers arrived when yellow fever had struck the city, as it had nearly every summer, but this time it was more severe. The sick, the suffering, and the dying were all around them. Many who could afford to do so left the city, but not the Flower family. Like Joseph Saunders, he did not let the epidemic stop him from fulfilling his priesthood. He did not spare himself day and night, calling on the sick and the dying and administering the Last Rites of the Church. He was prepared to give up his own life if that were the cost, and he did.

According to the *Pensacola Gazette*, September 10, 1853, David Dubois Flower died at half past eight o'clock on Saturday evening, and his funeral was scheduled for Sunday at ten o'clock. On September 17, 1853, the *Pensacola Gazette* paid tribute to him. "In the short ministration of less than three months, he had by his truly humble and affectionate deportment, and by the conscientious and earnest discharge of his sacred functions, won the deep respect and warm affection of his now lamenting flock. He died of the prevailing disease, a victim to his assiduous attendance on the sick beds of his parishioners."

In a letter written September 12, 1853, by Mrs. P. R. Anderson of Christ Church to a friend, we find her comments on Mr. Flower's death and the yellow fever epidemic. "Yesterday we buried our beloved Father the dear Mr. Flower, endeared to all even with so short a sojourn amongst us by his meet and holy life, his humility which he spoke in every word and action, his faithfulness to his church and all connected with it, and his unselfish and untiring zeal in going about among the sick and dying, praying, comforting, and helping them entirely unacclimated he spared not himself day or night if he thought he could be useful—until he was himself taken with the fever and fell a sacrifice to his duty. His poor

PART SIX, The Lost Rectors

wife is in deep affliction though humble . . . in hourly expectation of giving birth to her first child. I spent yesterday by her side, the first time I have left my children, and it was sad indeed. Sickness and death are everywhere around us. Scarcely a family has escaped and in several instances we have had three interments a day. At Warrington, the physicians say the mortality in proportion to the population is greater even than in New Orleans."

It is noted in the newspaper and vestry minutes that Mr. Flower was buried under the chancel of the church. The archaeological investigation in 1988 determined, however, that he was actually buried under the vestry room of the church and beside the Rev. Joseph Saunders. Mr. Flower's grave was the first of the three graves discovered on Tuesday, May 17, 1988, less than three inches under the ground. His grave had been disturbed, we assume, by the Union Troops who reportedly dug up the graves during the occupation of the city during the Civil War.

Shortly after his death, the vestry had a memorial marble tablet made in memory of Mr. Flower, and it was placed in the wall of the church. There was some discussion recorded in the vestry minutes as to whether Mr. Flower was to be called "Rector" or "Rector-Elect" since his canonical papers had not been received at the time of his death. The marble tablet reads "Rector" but his age at the time of his death on the tablet is wrong. He was thirty-one, not thirty-three.

The tablet reads as follows:

FAITHFUL UNTO DEATH
SACRED
TO THE MEMORY OF
REV. D.D. FLOWER
LATE RECTOR OF THIS
CHURCH
WHO DEPARTED THIS LIFE
SEPTEMBER 10th, 1853
AGED 33 YEARS

"HE BEING DEAD YET SPEAKETH"

ERECTED BY HIS CONGREGATION AS A TRIBUTE OF AFFECTION TO ONE WHO SACRIFICED HIS LIFE BY HIS LABORS AMONG THE SICK AND DYING; DURING THE PREVALENCE OF PESTILENCE.

He was also not forgotten at St. Luke's Church in Jacksonville, Alabama. In 1856, when St. Luke's Church built a small Gothic Revival church building, the altar windows were dedicated in memory of D.D. Flower with the following inscription: "In Memory of D.D. Flower, First Rector of This Parish, Died the fourth day before the Ides of September, 1853."

The story of the Rev. David Dubois Flower is one of success and sadness, one of triumph and tragedy. Very young, he founded two parish churches in Alabama, one in Jacksonville and one in Mobile. He served faithfully, always putting the priesthood above any other concern, even the possibility of his own death at such an early age. He had gone far in but six years from the time of his ordination as a deacon. His life had just begun, and in but one month, that fateful fall of 1853, the entire Flower family was wiped out by yellow fever. He never lived to see his son, born five days after his death. His story and the story of his little family is one of unselfish sacrifice. He was a faithful priest and pastor. He gave his life for his flock. He served the Lord he loved and the church he loved, and Pensacola and Jacksonville, Alabama, mourned the loss of this young man and his family they had come to love so deeply. "Greater love has no man than this, that a man lay down his life for his friends."

SOURCES AND ACKNOWLEDGEMENTS

1. **The Christ Church archives,** including the many volumes of Christ Church parish registers, vestry minute books, and collected writings of some of the former rectors of the parish; also newspaper articles going back to the days of the *Pensacola Gazette* prior to the Civil War. Most of this book could have been written just from this remarkable collection of valuable primary sources in the Christ Church archives.

2. **Newspaper articles** from the *Pensacola Gazette*, some in the Christ Church archives and some collected for me by local historian Mary Dawkins pertaining to Christ Church in the nineteenth century when she was doing graduate work at the University of West Florida. Also articles from the *Pensacola News* and the *Pensacola Journal* in the early part of the twentieth century from the Christ Church archives.

3. Material from **the Rev. Huston Horn**, an Episcopal priest and historian, of Pasadena, California, including a copy of a letter written by Joseph Saunders to his wife in Pensacola in 1836, the text of which is included in the biography of the Rev. Mr. Saunders, from the Perkins Library of Duke University.

4. **Ronald J. Caldwell, Ph.D.**, professor of history at Jacksonville State University in Jacksonville, Alabama, who provided me with information about the Rev. David Flower during his ministry at St. Luke's Church in Jacksonville, Alabama.

5. Several editions of the **Journal of the Diocese of Florida** in the Christ Church archives.

6. Information provided by **the Rev. McLaurine Hall,** historiographer of the Diocese of Florida, about the Rev. John Jackson Scott from the 1880, *Journal of the Diocese of Florida*, giving us the date of the Light of the World Window, a memorial to Bishop Francis Huger Rutledge.

7. Copy of portions of the **diary of Bishop Jackson Kemper**, Christ Church archives.

8. Various articles and notes from the eighteenth century about the visits of missionaries sent to Pensacola by the Bishop of London from the Christ Church archives.

9. *Christ Church Parish, Pensacola, Florida, 1827-1927*, Julia J. Yonge, privately published in 1927 on the 100th anniversary of the founding of the parish.

10. *Historical Sketch of the Church in Florida:* J.J. Daniel, Christ Church archives.

11. *A Goodly Heritage, The Episcopal Church in Florida 1821 to 1892*, Joseph Cushman, University of Florida Press, Gainesville, 1965.

12. *Early Churchmen of Florida:* George R. Fairbanks, Christ Church archives.

13. **Julia E. Randle**, archivist, Bishop Payne Library, Virginia Theological Seminary, Alexandria, Virginia, who supplied me with information about the matriculation dates of John Jackson Scott. "Catalogue of Officers and Students of the Protestant Episcopal Theological Seminary of Virginia," 1836-1837, and 1838-1839.

14. "The Southern Churchman," July 19, 1839, p. 3.; and May 7, 1841, Vol. vii, no. 15, p. 59, c.3; December 5, 1895, p. ll, c. 2-3; December 14, 1895, p. 782, from Virginia Theological Seminary.

15. **William and Mary College** *Quarterly Historical Magazine*, October 1923, Volume III, No. 4.

16. *History of the Protestant Episcopal Church in Alabama*, 1763-1891, Walter C. Whitaker, Roberts and Son, 1898.

17. *Virginia Cousins, A Study of the Ancestry and Posterity of John Goode of Whitby, from 1148-1887* by G. Brown Goode, C.J. Carrier Company, Bridgewater, Virginia, 1963, Virginia Theological Seminary.

18. *Pensacola, Florida's First Place City, A Pictorial History,* Jesse Earle Bowden, Gordon Norman Simons, Sandra L. Johnson, The Donning Company Publishers, Norfolk, Virginia Beach.

SOURCES AND ACKNOWLEDGMENTS 117

19. *The New History of Florida,* edited by Michael Gannon, University Press of Florida, 1996.

20. *Andrew Jackson And Pensacola,* James R. McGovern, Volume II, The Pensacola Series Commemorating the American Revolution Bicentennial, 1974.

I also express my grateful appreciation to Norman Simons, who for many years was curator of the museum at Old Christ Church and a staff member of the Historic Pensacola Preservation Board, who fed me information over the years about Christ Church and the history of Pensacola in the nineteenth century. I remember quite well one late afternoon in 1975 when I discovered a large wooden box in a closet at Christ Church, and inside I found more than 100 items dealing with the purchase of the property on which Old Christ Church was located, matters concerning the construction of the building in 1832, notes from the rector during the Civil War, and order forms for the stained-glass windows purchased in 1884 as well as other valuable information. Norman came to my office, and I had never seen him so excited. This information is in the Christ Church Archives as well as many pages of notes taken from conversations with him over the years which helped me greatly in the writing of this book.

I also am greatly indebted to Miss Lelia Abercrombie and her selected writings and notes taken from conversations with her over the years which are also in the Christ Church Archives. Much of this information I have shared with the Historic Pensacola Preservation Board, the Pensacola Historical Society, the University of West Florida John C. Pace Library, the archives of the Diocese of Florida, and the P.K. Yonge collection at the University of Florida for the sake of preservation.

I must also express my appreciation to the authors of those many books about the history of Northwest Florida and American history during the colonial and Civil War years, which I have read and remembered and long since forgotten titles and authors, but the contents became, as books always have for me, a part of my life.

This book would not have been possible without the support and encouragement of Earle Bowden, former editor of the *Pensacola News-Journal* who was not only an inspiration to me but a source of valuable information about the history of Pensacola during the nineteenth century; Dr.

Morris Marx, parishioner and president of the University of West Florida; and Braden Ball, former publisher of the *Pensacola News Journal*, who supported and encouraged me all along the way in the writing of this book and who, in many ways known only to the two of us, is responsible for its publication. I also owe a debt of gratitude to Tom Muir, historian for the Historic Pensacola Preservation Board, who read the manuscript, made many suggestions, and gave me help and support all through the process of writing, research, and revisions.

Two other friends and collegues spent many hours reading the manuscript and assisting me. This book would never have been possible without their help. Ginny Graybiel, staff writer for the *Pensacola News Journal*, was my "proof editor." I am also deeply grateful to Dr. Emory Thomas, regent's professor of history at the University of Georgia, one of the nation's leading authorities on Civil War history, who read the manuscript and offered valuable corrections and additions. Greater love hath no one than this, to read and work on someone else's book!

And finally, but not the least, I thank my wife, Eleanor, who suffered through the research, the long night hours of writing, and my preoccupation with my love of the history of Christ Church and Pensacola. Without her, this book would never have happened. Thank you, dear Eleanor.

BMC
Pensacola, Florida
Summer, 1998

INDEX

Abercrombie, Lelia, 63-65, 67, 76
Abercrombie, S. Cary, 64
African-Americans,
  in Pensacola, 22, 24
  ministry of Rev. Saunders, 98
  see also Zion Chapel this index
Alfred, A. D., 61
Anderson, P. R. (Mrs.), 112
Anderson, Walker, 24, 44, 45, 95
Anderson, Walker, Jr. (d. 1920), 45
Anderson, William Edward, 24, 44, 45, 54, 55
Apalachicola, Florida—Episcopal Church, *see Trinity Church (Apalachicola)*
Archaeological Search for Rectors
  archaeological project, 73-90
  excavation, 78+
  Flower grave found, 79-80
  funeral, reinterrment, 87-90
  groundbreaking (1988), 75-76
  identification of rectors, 86-87
Areson, Joseph, 53, 54
Avery, Albert L., 44, 46, 51, 53, 56

Baars, Henry, 53
Baker, W.H., 44
Banjanin, Tom, 75
Baskerville-Donovan, 69
Bell Property (purchased for Christ Church 1903-), 61
Bense, Judith A., 73
Bill, Silvester, 21
Blacks, see African-Americans; *see also Zion Chapel*
Blackwater, Florida, *see Milton, Florida*
Blocker, Edna Browning, litany desk memorial, 62
Blount, A.C., 44, 51, 52
Blount, A.C., Jr., 46

Blount, Frederick N., 46
Blount, Thomas M., 23
Blount, William Alexander, 46
Bluff Springs, Florida,
  episcopal mission church, 61
Bowden, Earle, 73-74, 77
Brosnaham, Hal Ashton, 64, 65, 66
Brosnaham, John, 20, 40, 42
Brown, Norborne A., 66

Caldwell, Ronald J., 110
Calhoun, John C., 27-28
  eulogy by Rev. Scott, 29-30
Cameron, John A., 23
  memorial tablet, 63
Chapman, George, Rev., 18
Chase, William Henry, 28-29, 40, 44
  death, 51

Christ Church (1832-1903) [Building]
Note: renamed "Old Christ Church" after 1903. See "Old Christ Church" in this index for later history of building.
  addition of tower (1879), 53-55
  archaeology, *see Archaeological Search, this index.*
  building and construction, 21-22
  during civil war, 37-42
  furnishings moved to new church in 1903, 62-63
  photographs, 54, 74
  pipe organ, 55
  report, condition after civil war, 45
  stain glass windows, 54, 55
Christ Church (1903-) [Building]
  construction, 61-62
  cornerstone laid (1902), 61-62
  furnishings from Old Christ Church, 62
  purchase of property, 61

120 THE SEARCH FOR THE LOST RECTORS

Christ Church (Pensacola)
    building consecrated (1836), 22
    first building constructed (1832), 21-22
    first ministers (1827), 21
    founding member of Diocese of Florida, 23
    incorporated (1827), 21
    land acquired (1827), 21
    move to Montgomery during civil war, 41-44
    period after civil war, 51+
    rectors, see Archaeological Search this index; see also names of individual rectors, this index.
    vestry organized, 21
Christ Church School, see Parish School of Christ Church
Church of England in Pensacola, 17
Church of the Holy Comforter (Montgomery, Ala.), 42
City of Pensacola,
    acquires Old Christ Church (1936), 65-66
    returns Old Christ Church, (1996), 67-70
Clubbs, A.V., 55
Cobbs, Nicholas H., Rt. Rev., 42
Coit, Emily, 64, 66
Colegate, Edward, 55
Collegiate Institute, see Pensacola Collegiate Institute
Cotton, Nathanial, Rev., 17
Cozzens, Mrs. E., 47
Crupper, M., 21
Currie, W.C., 66
Currin, Beverly Madison, text at groundbreaking of Archaeological Search, 75-77

Daily, Robert, Dr., 86-87
Daniels, John, 70, 74
Davis, John E. and Sarah, baptismal font memorial, 62
Dawson, William, Rev., 17
DeSilva, H.G., 64
Dorr, Eben Walker, altar rails memorial, 62
Drake, Edwin, 23
Duff, Eric (photo), 83
Dunn, J.W., 108
Durnford, Elias, 18
Duval, William P., 21

Easter Sunday
    —(1889), 56
    —(1903), new church, 62
Edwin, G. Weed (Bishop of Florida), 55
Elliott, Stephen, 41
Episcopal Bishop of London, 17
Episcopal Church
    in Confederate States, 41
    Domestic and Foreign Missionary Society, 21
    General Missionary Society, 20, 21
    reunited with northern church, 43
Episcopal Church (Florida)
    founding in Florida, 22-24
    history, 93, 96+
Episcopal Church (Pensacola)
    history, 17+

Fabbro, Mary Ann, 79
Flower, David Dubois, Rev.,
    arrival in Pensacola, 111-112
    biography, 110-114
    burial under chancel, 75
    called as rector, 32
    death (1853), 112-114

INDEX

funeral and reburial, 89-90
grave located, 79-80, 83, 87
memorial tablet, 62
Fort Barrancas,
    Episcopal chaplains at, 25, 30
Fort George, 18
Fort Pensacoola, 18
Fort San Miguel, 18
Freeman, Mr., 32
Gaines, Robert P., 69
Gonzalez, Manuel, 19

Haight, Charles C., 53
Hallmark, Daisy, 45
Hallmark, G.D., 66
Hallmark, George, 45, 76, 79-81
Harrison, Hendree, 64
Hinkle, Edmond R., 69
Historic Pensacola Preservation Board, 68, 70
Hodgkins, Henry Bell, Dr., 66
Hogeman, Wylie, 68, 69
Hutchins, Benjamin, Rev., 21, 93
Hyer, Henry (1792-1868), 44, 46, 55
Hyer, Julia (1796-1858), 55
Hyer, Louis, 44
Hyer, Louis, altar rails memorial, 62
Hyer, William Kopman, 46, 52, 54, 56
Hyer, William Kopman, Jr., 55
Hyer Family stain glass window, 55

Jackson, Andrew
    appointment as governor of Floridas, 19
    invasion of Spanish West Florida (1814-1818), 19
Jackson, Rachel, 20
Jerrison, John, 21
Joy, Deborah, 79
Judah, William H., 44, 46, 52, 55

Karadin, Ken, 89
Kemper, Jackson, Rt. Rev., 22, 96
Kerr, David, Rev., 31-32
Key West, Florida
    St. Paul's Church, 24
Keyser, Lovett, 66
Knowles, Josephine Hyer, altar cross memorial, 62
Knowles, Josephine Loring, hymn boards memorial, 62

Ladies Aid Society (of Christ Church), 55, 61
Lee, W.F., 52
Lewis, Rodman, Rev., 24

Magie, Roderic, 69
Marx, Morris, 75, 77
Maxwell, A.E., 44, 46
Maxwell, E.C., 66
Milner, Frank, 64
Milton, Florida,
    episcopal church established, 30
    see also St. Mary's Episcopal Church, this index
Mitchell, Robert, 21
Montgomery, Alabama,
    Church of the Holy Comforter, 42
Moody, Jim, 77
Morris, Ben, 87
Morrison, R. B., 66
Nelson, Don, 87

Old Christ Church (1832) [Building]
Note: Before 1903, this building was known as Christ Church; see "Christ Church (1832-1903)" this heading for earlier history.
    (1903-1928), used as St. Cyprian's

Episcopal Church, 62, 63
  (1928-1936), abandoned, 63
  (1929-1936), attempts to
    preserve building, 64-65
  (1936), deeded to City of
    Pensacola, 65, 66
  (1936-1959), used as public
    library), 66
  (1959-1996), used by historical
    society, 66
Old Christ Church Foundation, Inc., 69
Organ (pipe, 1887), 55-56
Overton, S. R., 21

Parish School of Christ Church, 42, 43, 47-48, 55
Peake, Charles Foote, Rev., 25, 105
Peake, Frederick Foote, Rev., 24, 107
  arrival in Pensacola, 104-105
  biography, 104-109
  burial under church, 75
  death (1846), 106-109
  funeral and reburial, 89-90
  identification of, 87
  memorial tablet, 62
Pensacola, Florida
  Christ Church, *see Christ Church this index.*
  description (1839), 96-98
  Episcopal Church, *see Episcopal Church, this index*
  history (1763-1781), 17-18
  history (1781-1821), 18+
  history (1861-1865), 37+, 76+
  Jackson invasion (1814), 19
  schools, *see Pensacola Academy, Pensacola Collegiate Institute, this index.*
  street names, 18

Pensacola Academy, 95
Pensacola Archaeological Society, 73, 77
Pensacola Colleagiate Institute, 25, 105
Pensacola Historic Village, 69
Pensacola Historical Society, 68
Pensacola Navy Yard, ministry at, 24
Perry, Edward Aylesworth, 40, 46
Phillips, John, III, 87, 89
Plaza Ferdinand, 18
Polk, Leonidas, 41
Powell, Gary, 10-13, 80, 89
Presidio San Miguel, 18
Preston, N.O, Rev., 31
Protestant Association of the City of Pensacola (1827), 20
Protestant Episcopal Church,
  organized in Pensacola, 20-21
  see also Episcopal Church
Roark, Mr., 65
Roberts, Mary Walthall Dorr, wooden eagle lectern memorial, 62
Rutledge, Francis Huger, Rev. (1st Bishop of Florida), 43-44
  death (1866), 44
  stained glass window, 54
Rutledge Memorial Window, 54, 55
Ryder, G.H. & Co., 55

Saunders, Joseph Hubbard, Rev., 22
  biography, 93-104
  burial under Vestry, 75
  death in 1839, 101-103
  funeral and reburial, 89-90
  identification of remains, 87
  letter to wife (1838), 99-100
  memorial tablet, 62
Saunders, Richard Benbury, 103-104
Saunders, William Laurence, 103-104
Scott, John Jackson, Rev., 25-26, 53

INDEX

at Fort Barrancas, 30-31
biography, 61
called back, (1855), 32-33
chaplain in C.S.A., 40
death (1895), 59
description of church upon arrival, 29
establishes church in Montgomery, Alabama, 42
memorial tablet, 62
named rector emeritus, 58
photograph, 27
resignation as rector, 56-59
Searle, Addison, Rev., 21, 93
Simons, Norman, 77
Slavery issue, 26-28
St. Cyprian's Episcopal Church, 61, 62
St. John's Episcopal Church (Tallahassee), 23
St. John's Episcopal Church (Warrington), 30, 61
burned by cannon shell, 41
condition after Civil War, 45
St. Joseph's Church (St. Joseph), 24
St. Mary's Episcopal Church (Milton), 61
St. Paul's Church (Key West), 24
St. Paul's Church (Quincy), 63
Stain glass windows, 54-55, 61
Steele, Ashbel, Rev., 22, 93
Sutcliffe, John, 61

Tallahassee, Florida; St. John's Episcopal Church, 23
Taylor, Al, 79
Temperance movement, 25
Trinity Church (Apalachicola), 24
Trinity Church (St. Augustine), 24

University of West Florida

Archaeological Institute, 73+
see also Archaeological Search
Warrington, Florida,
see St. John's Episcopal
West, Cindy, 77, 82
West Florida (British), Church of England in, 17
West Florida (Spanish), 18-20
Whaley, Percival Hanahan, Rev., 59, photo 60, 63
White, Joseph M., 21
White, W.W., 64, 66
Whiting, C.R. and J.C., credence table memorial, 62
Williston, Ralph, Rev., 20
Wilson, Henry, 21
Woman of Samaria (window), 55
Woolsey, Melanchton T., 21, 22
Wright, Benjamin Drake, 24, 46
Yellow Fever,
in death of Rev. Peake, 112
in death of Rev. Saunders, 100
Yonge, C.C., 44, 46, 52, 53, 55
Yonge, Chandler C., Jr, 47, 53
Yonge, Louise, 64
Yonge, Marjorie, 65
Yonge, Philip K., 47, 53, 56
Young, John Freeman (2nd Bishop of Florida), 53
death 55
Zion Chapel, 56, 61, 62